"With deep compassion, Chris [ ] hopeful story. He navigates the often-misunderstood intersection of mental health and spiritual well-being with hope and wisdom that are desperately needed in today's conversations about mental health in the church. I pray that Chris's vulnerability starts conversations among believers, church leaders, and families."

Kathi Lipp, author and podcaster, Clutter Free Academy

"Chris Morris is a voice the church needs to hear! By courageously sharing his story, Chris opens a much-needed conversation about mental health, weaving personal narratives, theological insights, and practical guidance into a topic that has long been left in the shadows of religious communities."

Marty Kaiser, campus pastor, Vineyard Church Reveal

"In this book you will encounter Chris as a wise guide who shares his journey's harsh and painful realities. As he skillfully unfolds his story, he encourages all of us to open ourselves to the beautiful possibilities for hope and healing in Jesus. May we all listen to Chris as he points us to Jesus, and may the church be filled with gritty friendships."

Rev. Dr. Gino Curcuruto, pastor, The Table Philadelphia

"Open this book and journey with Chris Morris in the struggle to make sense of mental illness within the Christian life. Read the stories, reflect on Scripture, and find hope. In these pages, Chris helps us see God as present in the struggle. *Resilient and Redeemed* is a gift to all of us who struggle with mental illness or walk with someone who does."

David Fitch, Lindner Chair of Evangelical Theology, Northern Seminary, Chicago

"If you are a Christian who battles with depression and suicide, this book is for you. If you have a loved one who struggles with these same elements, this book will help you understand their battle and how you can encourage and pray for them. Chris invites the reader into his very personal journey with reflection and understanding, and his words provide hope and healing through God."

Morgan L. Busse, award-winning author of THE RAVENWOOD SAGA and SKYWORLD series, and pastor's wife

"I ask my clients, 'Has your faith, theology, or church experience been helpful or harmful?' Chris vulnerably and courageously writes about how he has been harmed and most importantly how he has been helped, literally saved, by God and treatment. He shares how depression can affect marriages. It's real, honest, and hopeful."

Sovann Pen, host, *The Courage, Coaching and Counseling Podcast*; licensed professional counselor, A New Day Counseling Center

RESILIENT
AND
REDEEMED

RESILIENT
AND
REDEEMED

Lessons about
Suicidality and Depression
from the Psych Ward

CHRIS MORRIS

BETHANYHOUSE
a division of Baker Publishing Group
Minneapolis, Minnesota

© 2024 by Christopher Brian Morris

Published by Bethany House Publishers
Minneapolis, Minnesota
BethanyHouse.com

Bethany House Publishers is a division of
Baker Publishing Group, Grand Rapids, Michigan

Printed in the United States of America

Library of Congress Cataloging-in-Publication Data
Names: Morris, Chris, author.
Title: Resilient and redeemed : lessons about suicidality and depression from the psych ward / Chris Morris.
Description: Minneapolis, Minnesota : Bethany House Publishers, a division of Baker Publishing Group, [2024] | Includes bibliographical references.
Identifiers: LCCN 2023051053 | ISBN 9780764242427 (paper) | ISBN 9780764243288 (casebound) | ISBN 9781493446698 (ebook)
Subjects: LCSH: Mental health—Religious aspects—Christianity. | Suicide—Religious aspects—Christianity. | Depression in men—Religious aspects—Christianity.
Classification: LCC BT732.4 .M66 2024 | DDC 261.8/322—dc23/eng/20231214
LC record available at https://lccn.loc.gov/2023051053

This book contains original material as well as excerpts from previously published articles by Chris Morris:
Chapter 7: "Earthy, Gritty Friendships Kept Me Alive," November 2, 2021, *Fathom* magazine, Fathom-Mag.com/stories/earthy-gritty-friendships-kept-me-alive
Chapter 9: "How I Survived a Suicide Attempt," August 11, 2019, ChrisMorrisWrites.com, www.ChrisMorrisWrites.com/how-to-combat-suicidal-thoughts-a-personal-testimony/
Chapter 11: "You Can't Love Me. I Don't Even Love Me," July 12, 2022, *Fathom* magazine, Fathom Mag.com/stories/you-can-t-love-me-i-don-t-even-love-me
Chapter 12: "One Family's Recovery from a Suicide Attempt," December 10, 2021, KatieRDale.com, KatieRDale.com/one-familys-recovery-from-a-suicide-attempt/

Cover image by Shutterstock
Author photo © Carmela Joy Photography

The author is represented by the literary agency of Mary DeMuth Literary.

24 25 26 27 28 29 30   7 6 5 4 3 2 1

This book is for all my friends and family who have stood beside me through all the moments in this book, and who have never stopped loving me or wishing me the best. Without each and every one of you, I wouldn't be here to write this book.

CONTENTS

INTRODUCTION

What to Expect in This Book

First things first. I hope if you've picked up this book, you are safe. If this book finds you in a mental health crisis, do me a favor right now—set it down, pick up your phone, and call a friend. If you don't have a safe friend to call, dial 9-8-8, the mental health helpline. Please don't let another second go by without getting in touch with someone who cares deeply about this life moving forward for you.

If that's not you, I'm guessing you know what it's like to feel on edge or off-kilter. You've probably had some moments when you've wondered how the day will end. You're not alone in this. Mental health statistics in the last few years have been astounding. In the first year of the COVID-19 pandemic, the global prevalence of anxiety and depression increased by a massive 25 percent, according to a scientific brief released by the World Health Organization.[1] Since these figures only include those individuals who have sought help for their mental health, the actual numbers are

1. "COVID-19 pandemic triggers 25% increase in prevalence of anxiety and depression worldwide," *World Health Organization*, March 2, 2022, https://www .who.int/news/item/02-03-2022-covid-19-pandemic-triggers-25-increase-in-prev alence-of-anxiety-and-depression-worldwide.

even higher. This isn't just an American phenomenon—these are global numbers. Regardless of where you call home, life has become harder to deal with these days.

And it isn't just the pandemic. Even studies completed before COVID hit show a spike in mental health challenges. More than half of all U.S. adults (58 percent) and practicing Christians (54 percent) say that at least one relational or emotional/mental health issue impacts their most important relationships.[2] Anxiety and depression are the most common challenges to relational satisfaction, with more than one-third of practicing Christians saying one or the other (or both) impacts their close relationships.[3] A 2018 Cigna study of more than 20,000 U.S. adults revealed that "just under half of all those surveyed report sometimes or always feeling alone" and that 43 percent of those surveyed "sometimes or always feel . . . that their relationships are not meaningful."[4]

How do we use statistics like this? Where can we find God in the middle of—let's be honest and call it what it is—this mess?

The very first step: talk more about it. There's just not enough energy being expended on conversations about mental health in the church. Most churches still act as though mental illness occurs because of the odd exception instead of being a normal part of life. This assumption harms the people sitting in the pews every week. If something doesn't change, those in the mental illness community will stop participating in churches altogether, and that's a terrible prospect.

That's where this book comes in.

We're going to have a frank and open conversation about depression and suicidality, without fear or embarrassment or shame. We're going to investigate the darkness and find God.

2. *Restoring Relationships: How Churches Can Help People Heal and Develop Healthy Connections*, Barna Group, 2020, 12.
3. *Restoring Relationships*, Barna, 13.
4. "Cigna U.S. Loneliness Index," *Cigna*, 2018, 3, https://legacy.cigna.com/static/www-cigna-com/docs/about-us/newsroom/studies-and-reports/combatting-loneliness/loneliness-survey-2018-full-report.pdf.

News flash: I've struggled with depression and suicidality my entire adult life. There have been seasons when the pressure of these things lessens, but I'm always aware of them in the back of my mind. Always.

Despite this reality, I can trace the presence of God in my life. God has never given up on me, even when I've given up on myself. Certainly, I didn't always *recognize* God's quiet movement, like when I attempted suicide in 2020, but I know I just missed his whispers until after the fact.

The church needs to hear this message: God doesn't disqualify anyone because of a mental health diagnosis. He does not become disappointed or befuddled or angry with us because we're battling depression or anxiety. God doesn't shake his head and throw up his hands, even if we're admitted to an inpatient facility. God is in the business of qualifying people with murky motives, broken dreams, busted pasts, and messed-up lives. He accomplishes his goals through people, and there are no perfect humans to choose from, save Jesus, who sits at the right hand of the Father now, interceding on our behalf.

Indeed, we have been called to good works that God has ordained beforehand, and we have been perfectly crafted for these works based on the exact dimensions of our experience and expertise. But we can only engage in these works when we move past the fear and shame of our mental health diagnoses. That's the heart of this book: to empower you to move into wholehearted service for God, regardless of any mental health struggle or diagnosis you might have. And I truly believe that this can happen, both because of the witness of Scripture and because this is precisely what God has done in my own life.

> That's the heart of this book: to empower you to move into wholehearted service for God, regardless of any mental health struggle or diagnosis you might have.

What to Expect in this Book

Each chapter will share a vignette from my life, an episode in which my lifelong battle with depression raised its head. We'll take our time walking through these moments. After each vignette, I'll share what I learned from that experience and then share applications and reflection-and-discussion questions. We'll end with a verse and a short meditation focused on the steadfastness of God, the trustworthiness of his presence, his grand, unending love, and how nothing—not even a mental health diagnosis—can separate us from that love.

Will this book be the answer to all your mental health struggles? I wish! But we both know mental health is too complex for that. However, I anticipate your time in these pages could help you move forward in your journey with God and mental health in three distinct ways.

First, you'll see from my story that God doesn't disqualify anyone because of a mental health diagnosis, and that he continues to invest his love and care into our lives regardless of how healthy we might be. Second, you'll gain some specific skills to call upon when your mental health feels out of control. These skills are powerful antidotes to the all-too-familiar feelings of helplessness and despair that come with mental illness. Third, as you wrestle with the truth of God's love for you and practice using good tools, you'll develop a stronger sense of mental stability, growth, and equilibrium in your life. This may be a book you come back to more than once to relearn and remember its lessons.

Likewise, I have a threefold prayer for you as you read. First, I hope you'll be encouraged in your walk with Christ, with a deeper assurance that no diagnosis can keep you from intimacy with God. Next, I want you to find strength in the practices outlined in this book so that you feel less alone in your journey. Finally, I pray you'll find greater hope as you look toward a future in which your mental health does not define your life.

Three Quick Notes

I need to mention a few things before we jump into the vignettes. Number one: my memory isn't always perfect, so there's a chance that I'm misremembering something. I've done everything I can to run these moments by other people who were there, to make sure I'm not exaggerating or straight-up imagining things that happened, but it's possible something slipped through. Nobody can remember everything correctly, even if those recollections end up in a book like mine have here. It's not an intentional oversight.

Second, the book promises lessons I learned in the psych ward, and we will get there. However, this book walks through my life in a broadly chronological way, and my visits to mental health facilities are more recent developments. This means that the psych ward visits come later in the book, but I promise they are coming. I learned a lot of lessons along the way to the psych ward, which largely became clear for me during my stays, as I had time to ruminate on my lifelong struggles with depression and suicidality. So just trust the process and keep reading. You'll eventually get to the psych ward and resilience. There's a lot to walk through before we arrive at those moments in my life, though.

Third, I have created a video course on resilience specifically for the readers of this book. I cover topics like what tools you can use to access resilience in your life and whether resilience has limits. You can find the QR code to this course in the *Additional Resources* section of this book toward the end.

1

Meeting Jesus

*Then call on me when you are in trouble, and I will rescue
you, and you will give me glory.*

Psalm 50:15

My Story

In a moment of total despair, I cried out to the God I didn't even
believe in. "If you're real, God—whoever you are—you have seven
days to show me or I'm going to end my life. I don't see the rea
son to go on, so you better get to work. I'm not kidding. Seven
days, or else. Amen, I guess." I had turned fifteen a few months
prior, so some part of this was teenage dramatics, but some of it
pointed to deeper problems. I felt overwhelmed by my life, and I
needed something to change. I had to know some reason for my
life existed beyond the atheistic existence I'd been experiencing.

It's not that I had been raised in an antireligious environment,
but an ambivalent one. It was more like I needed to figure out on
my own what I believed about God, and my parents weren't that

concerned with giving me help on this topic. That's not a fair thing to put on a kid, so I chose not to believe anything. I figured God would show up if he wanted me to believe something different, and then I basically lived as though God didn't exist. While I carried a bit of a dark storm cloud over my head, I still felt like atheism worked out all right for me overall. I had some stuff to deal with from my parents' divorce and my dad's alcoholism, which I wouldn't deal with for a long time, but I got through most days without an emotional breakdown. As I said, I did all right—not great, but decent. Then the bottom fell out of my so-so life in an instant.

I woke up one morning to get ready for school and noticed my mom wasn't awake yet. That was odd because she usually walked out the door as I woke up. I went into her bedroom to see if she had just overslept, and I saw her on her bed in the middle of a seizure. "Mom, are you okay?" I asked. She came out of her seizure for just a moment and said, "Yeah, I'm just not feeling well. Check back with me in five minutes." Then she went back to seizing. Shaken to my core, I listened to my mom anyway. I grabbed some breakfast and wolfed it down, thinking the whole time about my mom and wondering what had happened. After I finished my meal, I went back to check on my mom. She remained in a seizure, but this time unresponsive.

I called 9-1-1.

"What's your emergency?"

"My mom is having a seizure that's lasted over five minutes and won't stop."

"Okay, we will send an ambulance to your house. Hang in there!"

A few long minutes later, the paramedics arrived and started checking my mom. "Does your mom use drugs?"

"No, she doesn't use drugs—why would you ask me that?"

"This looks like a drug overdose to me, that's why." (I look back on this and shake my head—who tells a fifteen-year-old his mom might be overdosing on drugs?)

For some reason, they didn't let me ride in the ambulance with my mom, so I found myself alone with a disaster of a house left by the paramedics, wondering if my mom would die or not. I didn't know what to do, and I couldn't think of anyone to call and ask for help, so I did the only thing that made sense—I went to school.

By the time I arrived at school, the first period had already started. I walked into the office to get a pass for class, and the office assistant asked me why I came to school late that day. I burst into tears and blurted out, "Because I think my mom might die!" The office assistant wisely got my school counselor, who asked me why I felt this way. I explained everything that had happened and then he drove me to the hospital. We found my mom's room. She had stopped seizing but remained unconscious. He stayed with me until we could get my mom's boyfriend on the phone, and he came to the hospital. My mom fought for her life over the next several days. Her temperature spiked to the degree that the doctors worried about brain damage or other permanent damage to her body. Several days later, the doctors released my mom from the hospital and things started to get back to normal for our family.

But not for me. If my mom, perhaps the kindest person I knew, could almost die at a moment's notice for no discernible reason, then what was the point of life? I continued to feel more and more desperation in my life as I explored all the religious systems of the world. I ran through Hinduism, New Age spirituality, Mormonism, Islam, and other less popular faith systems, but none made sense to me. I even considered Norse mythology! I needed to know the purpose of life, and I found myself increasingly desperate. So, I made my bargain with God. I didn't believe at that moment that God existed, and I certainly didn't expect him to be paying attention to me if he did. But the threat of suicide in seven days loomed large—I had a plan and an intent to execute the plan. I never thought God would use the stranger next door to change my life, but that's exactly what he did.

On day six after my plea for God to show up, my next-door neighbor whom I'd never spoken to knocked on my front door and invited me to her birthday party right then. I told her I didn't have time to come to her party. She peeked around me and said, "I think your Nintendo won't miss you if you stop by for an hour or so." I told her I didn't have a present, and she countered that she didn't need one from me. We went back and forth a few more times, and finally I capitulated, mostly because I couldn't think of any other excuses. I followed her back to her party with a bunch of strangers, expecting to leave about five minutes later. Instead, every single person I met overwhelmed me with kindness and genuine interest in me, to the degree that I said to someone, "I'm sort of a jerk. Why are you being so nice to me?" They replied that their kindness came from Jesus and that I should come with them to church the next day to learn more. Mostly because I hadn't explored Christianity yet and knew time was short on my bargain with God, I agreed to show up. This decision changed my life.

The next day, I went to church for the first time in I don't know how long. The youth pastor talked about Romans 8, and he ended with a powerful promise: "Nothing can separate any of you from the love of God in Christ Jesus, but only if you are in Christ Jesus. If you aren't in Christ, then the love of God isn't for you yet. It can be, but it's not activated yet."

He invited anyone who wanted to know more about this love of God to come up and talk to him. While he spoke about the love of God, my spirit burned inside me. I know enough now to know the Spirit of God wooed me to salvation, but I didn't know that then. I just knew that I needed to understand more about this Jesus.

I went up and talked to the youth pastor, and he shared the good news of the gospel with me. He told me I had sinned and deserved death, but that through the sacrifice of Jesus, I instead had the opportunity to have a close friendship with God. He asked me if I wanted that friendship, and I almost leaped out of my skin saying yes. At that moment, I prayed a prayer of salvation, and I can honestly tell you my life has never been the same. For a season, my depression and suicidality even lifted in the joy of my new spiritual life. It would return, but for a few years, I had the joy of being free from these burdens and felt the joy of growing and learning more about God.

What I Learned

God listened to the desperate prayer of a suicidal fifteen-year-old kid and orchestrated events so that I would hear just the right message on day seven of my bargain with God. He used a stranger who lived next door to me. He used a group of kind strangers I'd never met before. He used a youth pastor who happened to be preaching about the unconquerable love of God in Christ. At that moment, I learned that God cared intimately for me—yes, even busted and broken and messed-up me. I didn't miss the fact that God wasn't late in fulfilling his end of the bargain I had half-seriously made with him. Even though I wasn't actually expecting any God to show up, I had seriously planned to end my life. My mom had a gun. I knew where to find it and how to use it. I had planned to end my life in just one more day. Instead, God jumped into the middle of my reality and said, "No, Chris. I love you desperately. Don't end your life." He said this through a dozen people, and he didn't use those words even once, but I received the message loud and clear.

> *God jumped into the middle of my reality and said, "No, Chris. I love you desperately. Don't end your life." He said this through a dozen people, and he didn't use those words even once, but I received the message loud and clear.*

This message would form the core of my next five to seven years. I quickly slipped into a mode where I allowed the love of God to become the foundation of my life. In this season, I didn't battle any suicidal ideations and I had very few depressive episodes. Things felt fixed by a magical, kind, and loving Jesus, and I reveled in this newfound life and hope. Alas, things weren't meant to stay this way, and I eventually had to learn some hard lessons about how God saves us through our trials more often than he saves us from our trials. For this season though, the miraculous healing of my suicidality filled me with great hope for my future.

I pray for each one of you that God takes away your suicidality and depression, at least for a season, as he did for me. It's a glorious sense of freedom that I can't even find words to explain, and in some ways, I wish I still lived out of that freedom. I have learned much about the grace of God through the dark spaces I've walked through since this season ended, and there's a sense in which I wouldn't trade those lessons for freedom, but there's another sense in which I wish I had freedom rather than battle-tested faith, if I'm being honest.

Regardless, I learned that God will go to any lengths to draw someone to himself. In the eyes of most, I wouldn't even have been worth saving. I sometimes acted like an angry young man then, dissatisfied with the world, and I was literally a day away from my last day on earth. Yet God looked from the heavens and said, "I love that one and want to rescue him from his dark pit." And that's exactly what he did. Through a series of events that, in retrospect, are borderline ridiculous, God set the stage for my next season of hope and joy. I'm forever grateful that he chose to intervene in my life when he did. I would have missed so many moments of joy that I didn't know sat on my horizon—my wedding day, the births of my children, tender parenting moments, precious friendships that keep me afloat in very real ways in my dark times, and the list goes on. God saw a life worth rescuing despite all evidence to the contrary, and he acted. Hallelujah!

Why It Matters

What's the most important part of my story? It's not unique. God didn't do something that he's never done when he rescued me by orchestrating unlikely events to set the stage for my salvation. Quite the contrary, God regularly rearranges lives through circumstances that don't make any sense. He changed Peter's heart in an instant with a tremendous catch of fish and, in the process, turned Peter into a future church leader. He looked at a tax collector and saw a faithful disciple, then learned that Matthew had many friends who needed to hear the good news of the kingdom of God when Matthew threw a party for Jesus and the community. But one story stands out among the rest of these moments where God used seemingly unlikely situations to bring salvation—Cornelius. Cornelius and his household became the first Gentiles introduced to the gospel, so this story takes on special significance, and there's application beyond the historical fact.

We can read his story in Acts 10. We read that Cornelius was a kindhearted Roman officer committed to the Jewish way of living. He gave generously to those less fortunate than him and prayed regularly. So far, nothing seems too far off, but it's about to get weird, so I hope you're ready. At three o'clock in the afternoon, Cornelius had a vision where an angel walked toward him. As always happens when angels are involved, Cornelius became very afraid and asked what the angel wanted with him. The angel gave him unbelievably specific instructions on where to find Peter and to ask Peter to come to speak with him. When I say specific, I mean that the angel told Cornelius what city to find Peter in, whose house to look for him in, and how to find that house in the city. Cornelius did what the angel asked him to do by sending people to get Peter. Pretty crazy, right? Just hang on, there's more to this story.

As the people sent by Cornelius neared Peter's temporary abode, Peter had a vision from God. God communicated in this vision that he can make clean whatever he wants to make clean, even things previously considered unclean by the Jewish regulations. As Peter pondered the significance of this vision, Cornelius's servants showed up and asked him to come to talk to Cornelius and his household. The Holy Spirit told Peter to go with them without asking any questions, even though he, as a faithful Jew, would be going into a Gentile's house, which would be considered unclean. The next day, Peter traveled to Cornelius's house and began to share the gospel with Cornelius, and everyone gathered to listen to the good news. In the middle of his sermon, the Holy Spirit fell on the Gentile listeners, so Peter baptized them.

So what's the significance of this story, and why pay attention to it at all? It shows the lengths that God will go to bring good news. God sent an angel to talk to Cornelius, gave Peter a vision, spoke directly to Peter through the Holy Spirit, and interrupted a perfectly good sermon by filling these Gentiles with the Holy Spirit. He did all of this because he saw Cornelius and loved him. God will go to any length to demonstrate his love for one person. He did this for me, he did this for Cornelius, and he will do it for you too. Nothing can conquer the love of God.

How It Applies

1. If you have ever made a bargain with God, how did that end up? By the way, it's okay if your experience wasn't a dramatic salvation experience like mine was—sometimes God seems to specialize in absence, not presence, but we can't find the redemptive patterns in our lives if we don't ask the questions.

2. What experiences have you had where someone seemed to be a literal angel of God, sent to show you the tender mercies of God in your life when you needed it most?

3. In your walk with God, when have you felt his presence in moments of darkness, lightening the burdens you've been carrying and giving you hope to move forward, even for just one more day?

4. What went through your mind as you read about the lengths God went to just to capture the heart of Cornelius, especially the specific revelations he gave to Cornelius and Peter to make sure that Cornelius heard the good news of Jesus Christ?

5. Do you believe that God is as invested in demonstrating his love to you in your life? Why or why not?

What God Thinks

I see very clearly that God shows no favoritism.

Acts 10:34

It's easy to read this verse and understand it to mean that God doesn't play favorites, and there's truth in that statement. However, the grander picture is this: everyone is God's favorite. One of my early mentors in life used to always tell me, "You're one of God's favorites. Don't forget that!" I want to pass that message on to you as you're reading this book. You're one of God's favorites. He adores you with every fiber of his being and longs to see you walking in freedom and joy. More than that, he longs to see you reflecting the love and light of his Son, Jesus. Sometimes that longing means tough times, but sometimes it means orchestrating events in remarkable ways to demonstrate his love to you.

Consider this question. How would you live your life differently if you lived in full recognition of the idea that you truly are one of God's favorites? Too often we relegate ourselves to backseat believers who God tolerates or maybe perfunctorily loves, but we think he probably doesn't like us very much. Being one of

God's favorites punches this idea directly in the face and knocks it out cold. You're one of God's favorites. Period. End of sentence. There are no exceptions or caveats or conditions. He adores you the way you might adore your kids or your parents or your pets. Only more.

2

Man Up and Pray More

From the depths of despair, O LORD, I call for your help.

Psalm 130:1

My Story

I wish I could tell you that my depression and suicidality left me forever when I met Jesus in high school, but that's not what happened. I got through college without any major depressive episodes, and for that, I'm very grateful. I had a lot of stress during those years, but for some reason, I never fell back into my depressive habits. I think I found myself too enamored with the rapid-fire learning that happened at my Bible college. You see, I'm a left-brained person, so being in a place where I was learning new things every single day filled me with joy. Unfortunately, not everything I learned helped me in the long run, due to the specific brand of Christianity I learned about.

For example, I was taught that maturing Christian people should struggle less with mental, emotional, and social things

27

as they grow. Maturity in Christ should supersede depression, social anxiety, generalized anxiety disorder, and trauma because Jesus is the Great Physician. Don't misunderstand me here: I do believe that Jesus can and does heal us from the pains of our past and present, but only sometimes. For reasons that are often confusing and best left to the theologians, sometimes God leaves us in our sorrow despite our pleas for rescue. Sometimes he determines that it serves his purposes better to let us be in pain, perhaps to draw more Christlikeness out of us or to prepare us for a future season of ministry. Regardless of the reason, which we'll never know for sure on this side of heaven anyway, sometimes life gets hard, and it doesn't fit with the fancy, neat, sanitary theological systems that some Christians have set up for themselves.

About four years after I graduated from college, I found myself wondering why God didn't fit inside my theological box. I had constructed the box very carefully with lots of Scripture and quotes from the church fathers, but my life still felt like it was falling apart. I read my Bible and prayed daily. I led ministries in my church. I did all the right practices, but things remained off for me somehow. Some of this came strictly from circumstances—I got married right after finishing college early and inherited a two-year-old son. Being twenty when I got married, things weren't easy, mostly because I had graduated from college but not yet to adulthood. I needed to figure out how to set a budget and keep food on the table every night for my fledgling family, alongside stepping into stepdad and husband roles, plus a church leadership role. Let me just say this: it felt like a lot to manage all at once.

I began to feel the familiar tug of depressive episodes once again. It always started the same, with an internal question like this: *Just who do you think you are doing all these things? Do you really think you're qualified to be a husband, father, and church leader? You're a mess, and you need to stop everything now.* Of course, I didn't even know what stopping everything would mean, but the questions weren't intended to be taken literally. No, they were intended to instill doubt and uncertainty in me, and they accomplished their goal. You see, I didn't have enough understanding of how trauma and spiritual warfare work to see that these thoughts weren't necessarily my own, but that they could be the voices of the enemy or of those who had hurt me in the past. Instead, I just accepted these thoughts as mine and began to feel overwhelmed.

My theological constructs became harmful to me. I believed that maturing Christians shouldn't have battles with depression, but I didn't fit into this construct well at all. I practiced all the right skills to develop maturity as I led in my church, but I had depressive episodes. Clearly, I didn't belong on the leadership team, but I also found part of my identity and worth in my leadership responsibilities. What could I do? I didn't know, so I tried to pretend like the depressive episodes weren't happening. I tried to power through by sheer willpower. That didn't work, pure and simple.

I began to have a church face, where I had everything together, and a home face, where I found myself sometimes (not always) a mess. My wife, Barbara, got immeasurably frustrated with me. She saw I was inconsistent inside and outside the church because of this crisis in my faith that was epitomized by the bad theology I learned in college. Barbara began telling me after every episode of anger or of wanting to give up on life that I needed counseling, or at least I needed to talk to our pastor about my struggles. I couldn't bring myself to do this because it would be admitting failure. Sadly, a machismo undercurrent had been added to my bad theology, so now I also felt that so-called "real men" didn't need help from anyone to deal with their stuff. I wasn't willing to admit failure, so I resisted.

Things came to a head eventually. I don't remember the specific event, but I finally agreed with Barbara. Something had to change. I scheduled an appointment to speak with my pastor and instantly started regretting it. He wouldn't understand, I told myself. He would judge me as a worthless man and remove me from the leadership team. He would tell me that I needed to grow up if I battled depression because stronger Christians don't have these problems. In an unusual turn of events, I shared these worries with Barbara (I typically internalized all my fears at this point in our marriage), and she assured me I exaggerated my fears. No pastor worth their salt would tear down a church member clearly in such pain, but he would instead step forward with helpful advice or refer me to a counselor. Over the next couple of days, I chose to believe Barbara and kept my appointment. In retrospect, I wish I would have gone somewhere else instead. I am glad I listened to Barbara and talked to someone, but my pastor wasn't equipped to help me in a meaningful way.

I shared with my pastor the struggles that I had with depression. I explained that I largely maintained a false sense of togetherness when running church events, while at home I somewhat regularly blew up at my wife and son or sloughed off into the bedroom to be by myself instead of investing in my family. I shared that I read my Bible and prayed, but it didn't seem to be doing much. I told him that I had been suicidal before I became a Christian and hadn't struggled with it since, but I had started to worry it might make another appearance because I had started fielding some of those same worthless thought patterns from my suicidal teen days. He listened to me ramble for about ten minutes, and then he spoke five words I will never forget: "Man up and pray more."

That's all he said—basically, to man up and pray more. He explained that Christian men find themselves at the forefront of the spiritual battlefield because God holds us responsible for ourselves and our families. If anything bad happens to anyone in our family, it's our fault because God calls us to be the spiritual head of the family. He told me I had failed in my responsibilities at home, and that the devil took advantage of me because of my weakness. If

I gave any space to those intrusive thoughts, I sinned and opened the door for the enemy to wreck my family because of my own personal sin. The only answer to this dilemma remained taking up my calling as a biblical man, standing strong in the power that Jesus gives all Christian men, and praying more. He told me that if I just prayed more, my depressive thoughts would have no choice but to dissipate because they come from the devil and God is stronger than the devil.

What I Learned

I'm not sure to this day what my pastor thought he would accomplish with this sermonette he gave me, but I walked out of his office completely defeated. I had been praying already to overcome these thoughts, but to no avail. I had been taking up my calling as a biblical man, and it didn't matter. I had even been reading the Bible every day, and it seemed to make no difference. Still, the depressive thoughts overwhelmed me on a near daily basis, and I felt helpless before them. So I walked out of his office convinced that maybe I wasn't even a real Christian. Maybe my conversion experience hadn't been sincere. That's the only explanation I could come up with because obviously my pastor had to be right, so there must be something wrong with me. I sank further into despair, and the pattern continued for several years. I felt overwhelmed by my negative thoughts on a regular basis and acted out against these thoughts in anger or isolation toward my family.

Slowly, I learned an even unhealthier pattern and started to internalize these thoughts entirely. I didn't express my sense of failure to my family or to anyone else at all. I kept it a secret in my heart, so on the outside I appeared to be a functioning and healthy Christian leader, but that wasn't real. On the inside, I continued to deteriorate into a train wreck. With my self-confidence shaken beyond anything I could repair on my own, I still doubted whether my faith was real. Nevertheless, I found some joy in leading things at church, so I pushed forward while always doubting the reality of my faith.

I also learned that Christianity isn't a safe space for mental problems. I made an unconscious decision to lock that part of my interior life away behind several doors and never to share anything about it again with anyone. This locked-door mentality would stay in my life for over a decade, much to my detriment and the suffocation of my self-development. I bought the lie that spiritual maturity and being mentally healthy are the same thing, and it kept me from growing mentally for a very long time.

In other words, nothing redeeming took place in the immediate aftermath of this vignette in my life. All my worst fears came to fruition when I talked to my pastor about my mental health struggles, so I learned to keep it all to myself moving forward. I include this story in the book because I think it's a relatable moment for many. Too many churches and church leaders have an oversimplified view of mental health and faith, rather than recognizing the nuanced reality that mature people can be (for example) depressed without their depression calling into question their faith. This theological construct has damaged so many people, and (some) churches are just now starting to come out of this pattern of belief.

Now I see something that I wish I had seen then, and it's worth sharing with you now. My then-pastor displayed signs of being someone who wasn't safe to talk to about my mental health issues. He regularly painted maturity in Christ as a black-and-white issue, as something you either had or didn't have, rather than the continuum that Scripture portrays it to be. He never talked

> *I bought the lie that spiritual maturity and being mentally healthy are the same thing, and it kept me from growing mentally for a very long time.*

about mental health concerns from the pulpit, unless he vilified the people battling them. He didn't even talk about moments of anxiety or depression as part of the normal course of life as we walk in this busted world. In retrospect, these things should have helped me to see that this pastor couldn't be a safe person to talk to about my depression and suicidal ideations. We will discuss this more in a later chapter, but it's vital to point out now that we can and should begin to figure out how safe someone might be *before* we share our struggles with them. Being a pastor or a counselor or a social worker doesn't equal safety—it's just not that simple, unfortunately.

Why It Matters

The other reason I shared this vignette from my life is that it's necessary to address this poor theology directly rather than hide from it. Too many people have been damaged by well-meaning pastors espousing so-called "biblical counseling" who share advice similar to my previous pastor's words. These pastors hurt their flock because they don't understand the full message of the gospel about mental health. Mental health does not equal spiritual maturity, and spiritual maturity does not guarantee mental health. There are many ways to approach this truism, and we will address it from many perspectives throughout this book, but right now I want to focus on what might seem a weird place—the apostle Paul.

Many of us are familiar with the apostle Paul. He's the guy who started most of the first churches. Along with Timothy and Luke and Barnabas and others, he went on three missionary journeys where he established churches in cities across the known Roman world. He also wrote about half of the New Testament. For Paul, it all started with a miraculous intervention from Jesus himself. Paul zealously defended Judaism, and as such, Christianity made him angry because he felt it misrepresented his faith. He literally had a letter from the high priest authorizing him to torture and potentially kill anyone who claimed to be a Christian, and then everything changed in an instant. Jesus appeared to him in the middle of the road, told Paul to stop persecuting the church because it held the truth, and struck him blind. He would eventually regain his sight and, along with it, a new passion for Jesus. He spoke of this conversion no less than three times to Roman officials in great positions of power, so it became a foundational and miraculous moment in his life. In other words, Paul was the real deal.

But then we come across this moment in 2 Corinthians 1:8 (NIV), where Paul says, "We do not want you to be uninformed, brothers and sisters, about the troubles we experienced in the province of Asia. We were under great pressure, far beyond our ability to endure, so that we despaired of life itself." Let's get real for just a moment now. If you received a letter or a text from a friend and they said they "despaired of life itself," you'd be worried. You would start wondering if suicide was on their mind. You would probably call that friend right away or go visit them. But the apostle Paul used this phrase. The man who started most of the first churches and looms larger in the New Testament than anyone except Jesus seems to be at least severely depressed, and maybe even suicidal. If Paul had this experience while planting churches across the known world, it's evident that maturity and mental health aren't always bedfellows.

But Paul teaches us more in this passage. He finds a hope that we must grasp hold of to see his secret for surviving this dark night of the soul experience. Second Corinthians 1:9–10 (NIV) continues with Paul's story:

> Indeed, we felt we had received the sentence of death. But this happened that we might not rely on ourselves but on God, who raises the dead. He has delivered us from such a deadly peril, and he will deliver us again. On him we have set our hope that he will continue to deliver us.

Do you see the beautiful contrast between the circumstances Paul faced and how God reacted to them? Paul felt he had received the sentence of death, but God allowed these circumstances so that Paul would rely on the God who *raises the dead*. And who would be included among the dead at this moment? None other than Paul himself! The promise of God in the middle of Paul's busted-up and broken life, in the very moment when he felt the deepest despair, remained—God would resurrect him because that is what God does. God resurrects dead things. He did it with Jairus's son, he did it with the widow of Nain, he did it with Lazarus, and most importantly, he did it with Jesus. God resurrects dead things, and this includes us. Paul ends his cry of despair with a modicum of hope and declares that God will continue to deliver him. We can join Paul in this declaration that God will continue to deliver us.

How It Applies

1. If you have ever talked to a pastor about your mental health, how did that go? If you haven't talked to a pastor about this, why not?

2. Have you ever come across the theology that mature Christians don't struggle with their mental health, and what did that emotionally feel like for you?

3. What emotions stir in you as you consider the idea that Christianity isn't always a safe space for mental health issues to be discussed?

4. When did you last despair of life itself, and who or what pulled you out of that moment?

5. How does it encourage you that God resurrects dead things and that even the apostle Paul needed God to resurrect his dead hope?

What God Thinks

He has delivered us from such a deadly peril, and he will deliver us again.

2 Corinthians 1:10 NIV

This verse sits in the middle of a New Testament lament. Laments are far more common in the Old Testament, but this fits the pattern perfectly. In a lament, four specific things happen. There is an address to God, a description of the complaint to God, a request for God's help, and an expression of trust in God despite the circumstances. Paul implies the address to God in the text, and the rest of this small passage perfectly represents a lament. Laments have multiple, powerful benefits for us in our faith, but let's start with the idea that God can handle our complaints. Too often we have been taught that God doesn't want to hear us complain, but nothing could be further from the truth. Our God wants us to be real with him, and that includes complaints.

Now onto the benefits of laments. Laments show that we know our help can only come from God, not somewhere else. By addressing our laments to God, instead of someone else or to the great void, we demonstrate that we know our help comes from God. We also release faith to continue to trust in God, regardless of the circumstances. Scripture continually tells us that faith comes through hearing or through action, and lament has elements of both.

We additionally call upon God to act in accordance with his character and his declared goodness toward us and enact anticipatory praise. We remind God of who he has promised to be, and in the Bible, we see many times where God responds to this type of interaction with others. We can also release our emotions—fear, anger, and uncertainty, among others—rather than holding them in and letting them fester. Emotionality shared with appropriate sources can be cathartic, and there's no better person to share our struggles with than God.

We give ourselves an antidote to fear by reminding ourselves that God is for us. Life often seems to conspire against us, telling us that God is either not for us or at best doesn't really pay attention to what's happening in our lives, but lament reestablishes the priority of God's heart for us. Finally, we invite God into our pain. As with anyone else, an invitation into our pain lessens our experience of that pain because we share the burden. Who better to share our burden with than the God of the universe? Each of these benefits should encourage us to engage God in a more real way when we hit our own dark nights of the soul.

Now it's time for a few more questions for you to consider related to lament. Have you ever composed or verbalized a lament to God, where you expressed your frustration with his apparent absence and called him to action? Do you have any reservations about taking this nearly aggressive approach with God? What do you think might happen if you stepped into a period of lament toward God—does it scare you, and if so, why? I want to encourage you to step past any hesitation you have and engage God in a lament-type of prayer. You will find your faith bolstered, and often you might even realize a better vision of what God could accomplish through a difficult season of your life.

3

My Pastor Took Antidepressants?

When I kept silent, my bones wasted away through my groaning all day long.

Psalm 32:3 NIV

My Story

Several years had passed between this chapter and the last. We had left the church I spoke of previously and found ourselves in a healthier community. This pastor did all the things that I mentioned my previous one never did—he spoke about mental health from the pulpit, he talked about Christian maturity as a continuum where we might slide forward and back in different seasons of our life, and he never belittled people battling mental health conditions. For the first time in a long time, I started to feel safe in a church environment. Then my pastor said something that both shook me deeply and opened long-closed-off parts of my life to the life-giving nurturing of Jesus.

Our pastor spoke that day about burnout in pastoral ministry from a place of real transparency. He said that the last few years had been a struggle for him because he took it very hard every time someone left the church, as though they judged him personally unworthy as a pastor. He shared that he had nearly stepped away from the ministry because it became too complex emotionally for him to endure. Then he dropped a bomb, the last thing I ever expected to hear a Christian pastor say, and certainly not the lead pastor of a church. He said, "I take antidepressants and boy am I glad I do—I need them."

I will never forget my immediate reaction to hearing him say this. I had several things going on in my brain and body all at the same time. For starters, I almost jumped out of my seat as I sat up quite dramatically. It's not that I wasn't paying attention to the sermon before, but now I needed to pay special attention to what came next. A sense of hypervigilance took over my senses as I awaited what I assumed would be the inevitable disclaimer. Something like, "Well, I used to take antidepressants, but as I've grown in my faith, I have realized I don't need them anymore." Or maybe, "I'm taking these pills now, but I look forward to the day that I will be free of them as I mature more." Or even, "Because of this necessity in my life, I'm stepping down as the lead pastor of your church, because pastors shouldn't be on psych meds." But I didn't hear any of that. Instead, I heard him say something like this: "For whatever reason, my body needs help to regulate all my emotions and my responses to the curveballs life throws at me as a pastor. My wife and my kids would be the first to tell you that I'm a much happier person on antidepressants. I'm also a better husband, father, and pastor on these pills." He went on to say that he knew some people would think less of him for being on the meds, or even for talking about being on them, but he didn't care because he had nothing to hide.

As I listened to him talk freely and share his journey with psych meds, I began to hear the whispers of the Holy Spirit in my own heart. His whispers sounded a lot like this—*If your pastor isn't ashamed of his meds, why are you hiding your meds from everyone you know as if it's a deep, dark secret?* You see, I had finally capitulated after several more years of battling anger and isolation silently and agreed to try some meds for my depressive episodes. I didn't tell anyone, though. I even asked my wife to keep it a secret from everyone, so nobody knew I took psych meds. I still believed that it proved my immaturity, and I didn't need other Christians thinking less of me. I knew I needed the medication, but I felt a trickle of shame every evening when I took my pills. I couldn't handle judgment from others when I already felt enough guilt on my own. I began to entertain these promptings from the Holy Spirit. How would my life look different if I stopped hiding this piece of my life from my friends and the rest of my family? More specifically, what might be the fruit of transparency in my life, rather than hiding in shame?

As the Holy Spirit whispered to me, I experienced two simultaneous and conflicting emotional responses. On the one hand, I felt hope begin to bubble up in my soul. Perhaps it would be possible to be freed from the terrible weight of shame and secrecy I had been bearing on my own (except for Barbara). Maybe I didn't need to worry any longer about editing my stories with my friends to make sure that I didn't disclose this terrible secret that I held. I wondered what it might look like to share this burden with people I already implicitly trusted, who I believed were members of Team Chris and rooting for me to succeed. On the other hand, I felt the judgment and shame rise up stronger than ever before. *Just because your pastor shares his sins from the pulpit doesn't mean you should do the same with your friends. Who knows how they will respond? Are you ready to lose friends over this secret, when it's perfectly safe inside your heart and with your wife? Why risk it?*

After the service, I talked over all of this with Barbara. She found herself surprised that I could even be open to the idea of talking to my friends about my psych meds. I asked her point-blank, "Do you think it would be okay if I stopped hiding the fact I'm taking antidepressants?" She chuckled a little, bless her kind heart, and said that of course it would be okay. She'd only been joining me in hiding this from others at my insistence, and it made her a little uncomfortable. I would like to say that I immediately started sharing that I took antidepressants because of my newly discovered freedom thanks to my pastor's own admission, but that isn't how this story goes. I wrestled with this for another couple of months, really trying to figure out if I would still be considered a decent Christian after talking about this myself. What if my pastor made a mistake in sharing his own struggles, and what if the outcry from his admission came soon? Why would I want to submit myself to the same scrutiny that he could be facing?

Eventually, I started timidly sharing with my close friends that I took antidepressants. I received absolutely zero judgment. Nobody had even an inkling of negativity about it, as a matter of fact. Some of my friends said that they had noticed a shift in my attitude toward life and wondered where it came from, but just never got around to asking. Others simply said they were happy I had found the help I needed. Across the board, every single friend I shared with asked me some form of this question: "Why did you hide it for so long, and why did you believe that I would judge you?" I found myself surprised and grateful for the friends God had placed in my life and relieved that I didn't have to filter my life experiences with them any longer. Instead, I could share freely about things that did or didn't work with my medication. I discovered that many of my friends also used medications for anxiety, depression, or ADHD, and we found new camaraderie in our shared experiences. In the end, I grew closer to my friends because I chose to be honest about this issue in my life.

What I Learned

This season became a powerful one for me, as I learned to step away from the shame and secrecy I had been carrying for nearly a decade and as I stepped into the light of transparency and community. The most important thing I learned through these moments is that the enemy of our souls hates when we engage in community. It's terribly hard to find people who can be trusted with the darkness we all carry within us, and it's a topic we will cover at length in a future chapter, but let me just say this for now: taking the risk of rejection and finding a true, safe community is one-hundred-percent worth the risk. I've built my life on a stronger foundation now that I'm more open with some key people in my life about the mental health challenges I have. I will also talk more about how these friends literally saved my life in a future chapter, but it's worth mentioning here that a safe community is worth every risk it entails, and it truly is lifesaving.

I also learned to be more careful about the theology I accepted into my head and heart. Sometimes the subconscious aspects of our theological understandings are the most dangerous parts of what we believe. This certainly became the case for me. At no time would I have ever told anyone else that they needed to have their mental health together for God to use them, but I nevertheless battled whether I could even be a Christian because of my own depression. There are so many theological traps we can fall into (many of them set unintentionally by our church leaders) that evict freedom from our lives and sequester us to places of dejection and fear. We must learn how to question the things we have accepted as true in our minds and hearts. It's a tricky exercise because it can almost feel like you're choosing not to submit to your church leadership, but there's so much value in undertaking this.

One final thing I learned: most people are kinder than we give them credit for. I worried about losing friendships. I raised the internal stakes of my decision to share my medication situation with my friends, but it wasn't an issue in any way. Indeed, every single one of my friends expressed gladness that I was eventually honest with them because it meant I didn't have to bear the weight of this alone. There are certainly unsafe people out there, and we must be careful not to cast our pearls before swine, as Scripture says (Matthew 7:6). Let me say this though: there are far fewer swine out there than we're likely to imagine. Most people want the best for others and will be generous in their responses to our pain, just like we would be kind in response to someone else's pain.

Why It Matters

Following my pastor's admission, what the Holy Spirit led me to in this season is, simply put, freedom. Freedom always indicates or leads the way to where God is moving in our lives. Second Corinthians 3:17 says, "For the Lord is the Spirit, and wherever the Spirit of the Lord is, there is freedom." God always offers freedom from bondage to his beloved children because we too often put ourselves in prisons of our own making. God always looks to draw us to freedom, every day and in every way.

Now let me clarify something here, because there's a danger if we aren't careful with our application of this idea. We have to take this verse in context, so let's look at the next verse: "So all of us who have had that veil removed can see and reflect the glory of the Lord. And the Lord—who is the Spirit—makes us more and more like him as we are changed into his glorious image" (2 Corinthians 3:18). So what does that even mean, right? It means that our road to freedom should always result in us reflecting the glory of the Lord and his glorious image more and more. If the freedom we are feeling called to looks sinful or damaging to others, then that offer isn't from God. But if the freedom we are feeling called to takes us farther down the path to reflecting the

> *When we're transparent with one another, we both love God well and give our neighbors a chance to love us well.*

lifestyle and priorities of Jesus, then it's a freedom we should be stepping into.

One key component of the freedom God calls us to is transparency. Perhaps the strongest indicator of this reality can be found in Galatians 6:2: "Share each other's burdens, and in this way obey the law of Christ." There are several things to unpack in this single verse, so let's get to work. For starters, it's impossible to share a burden with someone who won't share. This verse implies or assumes that we are being transparent with each other, or it doesn't even make any sense. So, the Bible assumes we become honest about the things burdening our hearts. These burdens could be financial, emotional, familial, mental, or anything else—the Bible tells us to share them. The second part of this verse might be even more important though, because it gives us the why behind the transparency. We obey the law of Christ by sharing our burdens. But what does "the law of Christ" mean? The most obvious answer could be the twofold answer Jesus gave when a Pharisee asked him about the most important commandments in the Bible. He said to love the Lord with all you've got and to love your neighbor as yourself. In other words, when we're transparent with one another, we both love God well and give our neighbors a chance to love us well.

To state this differently, every time we choose against transparency, we choose to step farther away from the best that God has for us. We actually choose to neglect our love for God, and we are refusing to let our neighbors love as they would love themselves. That puts quite a different spin on things, doesn't it? We can find one hundred instances in the New Testament of the Greek word translated "one another," and nearly sixty of these instances specifically tell us how to relate to others.[5] We are broken beings who want to hide behind our sorrow and shame, but God always calls us to freedom and transparency because it's the path to finding God's best for us.

How It Applies

1. How would you respond if you heard a pastor say he took antidepressants because he needed them, or if you have heard that, how did you respond?

2. How afraid are you to share your mental health struggles with your friends, and what are the specific fears that cross your mind when you consider being more honest about your battles with mental health?

3. What steps toward freedom might the Holy Spirit guide you toward in this season of your life? What keeps you from stepping into that freedom?

4. How difficult do you find it to share your burdens with your neighbors in Christ? Does it become more difficult with some burdens—financial, social, familial, etc.—than others, and why?

5. If you had to define God's next best step for you right now, what would you say? How is it related to freedom and transparency?

What God Thinks

For the Lord is the Spirit, and wherever the Spirit of the Lord is, there is freedom. So all of us who have had that veil removed can see and reflect the glory of the Lord. And the Lord—who is the

5. The Greek word is *allelon*. A perusal of any Greek lexicon will show you that this word occurs exactly one hundred times in the New Testament. I did a word study of this term and its appearances in the New Testament to determine how many instances relate to how we interact with each other.

Spirit—makes us more and more like him as we are changed into
his glorious image.

2 Corinthians 3:17–18

We all have areas in our spiritual and mental lives where we don't
allow freedom to reign. I'd like you to take a minute or two and
think about these questions: Where are you most hindered in your
faith walk with God? The way you think about your own use
of psychiatric meds? Do you believe as I once did that only the
immature struggle with their mental health? Do you think God
waits to jump on you with judgment and fury if you open up
about your struggles? Do you feel hindered in being open with
your fellow Christians about your battles because you fear the
loss of a relationship?

It might be none of these things, but you probably know exactly what it is. If you're anything like me, you've been thinking
about it off and on for some time, and you wish it would go
away, but it never seems to leave. We are going to attack this
shackled-up part of your life right now, and we're going to do it
with faith and gusto. Don't worry—if you lack faith that God
will honor any change you're looking for, you can borrow my
faith. I will be for you like the friends who lowered the paralyzed
man through the roof to get to Jesus. We've got this covered,
together—trust me.

Join me in prayer. Consider this prayer a guide for you to interact with the God of freedom; you can modify it however you
want to fit who you are. You don't have to repeat it word for word,
though you certainly can if you want to.

*Father, I believe you are the author of freedom, and I believe
you long for me to walk in your freedom. I'm not doing
that right now because I can't seem to let go of [insert your
struggle here]. I've tried to before, but it just hasn't worked.
I'm coming to you again and asking you for freedom. Would*

you teach me to walk in your grace and freedom in this area, so that I can recognize the presence of your Holy Spirit in my life in new and exciting ways? I don't want to be hindered anymore. I want better for myself, and I know you do too. Teach me to step into the newness of freedom, starting right now, Lord. In Jesus's name I pray, Amen.

4

That Just Stinks

*Share each other's burdens, and in this way obey the law
of Christ.*

Galatians 6:2

My Story

Weird name for a chapter title, right? Hang tight for just a moment and you'll see why it's the perfect title in just a few minutes. I unexpectedly received a call from one of my best friends in the middle of the day. It struck me as unusual because he works, so we usually only text during the day. I picked up the line and heard Kevin crying on the other end. "Dude, what's wrong?" I asked him.

"My dad just died."

I didn't know what to say. His dad had had some struggles over the last few years, but who doesn't as they get older? Nothing prepared Kevin for this, though. I wrestled with what to say for a few minutes. I mumbled an "I'm sorry" and asked how it had happened. He explained the details behind his dad's death and then asked, "What am I supposed to do? I'm not ready for my dad to be gone, Chris."

I still didn't know what to say. You see, I haven't experienced a lot of death involving close family members in my life, so I found myself ill-prepared for this conversation. Here's what I knew I couldn't do though—I couldn't offer Christian platitudes to my best friend as he grieved the sudden loss of his father, when he needed comfort. But I didn't have any comfort to offer him, so I said the next thing that popped into my head: "Dude, that just stinks. I'm so sorry. I don't even have words that will do justice to what you must be feeling, but I'm here for you." At this, Kevin burst into even deeper sobs, gut-wrenching sobs that seemed to come from his very soul. I listened on the phone for probably another five minutes as he cried, then he said he needed to go.

In the moments following that call, I actually felt a bit useless. I wanted to be able to offer my friend more than a meaningless comment, which I felt I had given him. This sense of uselessness stayed with me for a while and even impacted my friendship with Kevin, as I presumed that I had let him down. As his best friend, I had nothing to offer him in one of his greatest times of need. Eventually, he noticed that I had pulled back some from our friendship, and he asked why we weren't as close as we used to be. I confessed that I felt I had been less than helpful when he shared about his dad's death. What he said stunned me then and, if I'm honest, it still surprises me today.

Kevin said that he talked to a bunch of people that day—family, friends, pastors, and coworkers. He received a lot of comments from everyone, but almost nothing helped. Plenty of people said, "At least he's in a better place now." Several said, "God has his reasons for this, and it will become clear in time." A few even said, "God has one more angel." Only one person said, "That just stinks," though: me. He told me that became

> *There isn't always an explanation for hard things, and it's okay to sit in sadness and breathe it in instead of looking for a clean answer to explain it away.*

the most helpful response he got from anyone that day and in the days since. After hearing so many unhelpful things, he started to feel as though he shouldn't even be sad over losing his dad. He said it seemed from others' responses that this should roll off his back like a minor issue. But this wasn't a small thing; his dad just died unexpectedly.

My response gave him permission to grieve. When I said it stinks, he realized that there isn't always an explanation for hard things, and it's okay to sit in sadness and breathe it in instead of looking for a clean answer to explain it away. He said that it unleashed a deeper sense of grief that he didn't realize had been sitting there needing to be expelled, waiting for a release. We've talked about this since, and it's been almost a rallying cry for him when he's overcome by grief again over his dad's death. Moments will unexpectedly hit him hard in the gut, and he will be left wondering afresh why his dad had to die so young. When he's reeling from the punch to the stomach, he remembers my fumbling comment—that just stinks. It gives him the courage to stand amid the grief and let it wash over him, instead of hiding from it or allowing shame to come instead of grief.

He's even used this comment with some of his other friends in their crises. Instead of feeling like he needs to have an answer to an impossible situation of sadness, he can enter into his friends' sadness with compassion and without answers. Let's be honest—nobody looks for an answer when they're in the middle of a tumultuous event. They want to know they're heard and that they aren't alone. Kevin has told me that he feels like saying "that really stinks" gives him a way to commiserate with his friends in a meaningful way without having to give false platitudes or explanations.

What I Learned

This might seem as though it's not related to depression or suicidality, but let me explain how it's actually intimately related to both. Sometimes circumstances cause our mental health to take a dive, like with my friend Kevin and his dad's death. Grief takes a lot of different forms though, and it's not always caused by a death. We can grieve the loss of a job, the loss of a friendship, the loss of a dream, or even the loss of a life once hoped for. In these moments, depression and suicidality lie to us. They tell us that our emotions are out of whack and that we shouldn't be responding with as much depth as we are feeling. They tell us we are wrong or over-reacting and need to get ourselves in order and be stronger. Men struggle with this specifically because toxic masculinity tells us lies like "real men don't cry" or "emotions demonstrate weakness." Against these false words, we have to find the courage to stand firm and feel our feelings. This can happen in a variety of ways.

In Kevin's case, it happened through my "that just stinks" comment. He felt the strength of his emotions for this very real, very painful moment instead of hiding behind a false sense of God's goodness or his ultimate purposes. He sat in his grief and allowed it to swallow him for a while. Kevin had a lifetime of memories to process alongside the reality that there would be no new memories to be made with his dad. He had to come to grips with the idea that he would never get to have a Saturday morning breakfast with his dad again, just sitting together and sharing life. His kids would never have another chance to interact with their grandpa again. Christmas would never be the same because his dad would never be there for another holiday.

Too often, especially in Christian circles, we are taught that emotions are dangerous and something to be kept under control.

We might be given space to grieve over the death of a loved one, but certainly not any of the other losses we talked about above. Yet, there are moments when the only right response might be to feel all the feelings that are overwhelming us. It's actually healthy to allow ourselves to wallow in grief for a season if there's real grief to be felt. Denying these emotions means we are making a choice to be dishonest with ourselves, which sets us up for later problems.

If we choose to ignore the deep-seated emotions of our difficult circumstances, we will find those emotions seeping out unexpectedly at other times. Perhaps our anger will erupt on our children over a small mistake, or aggravation will trickle out inappropriately into our workplace. Here's the truth: emotions don't just disappear. We have to process them one way or another. We have the choice as to how we want to process them, directly or indirectly. If we choose indirect processing, though, then we won't find emotional wholeness because we aren't dealing with the root cause of the deep-seated emotions.

When circumstances come at us with the fury of a thousand summer suns, we have to choose to look them straight in the face and address them. There's no easy way through them, but the end result makes it worth the effort. We can look at these circumstances and give ourselves permission to feel the feelings and banish the lies that say we ought not to feel things so deeply. When we do this, we create a barrier of sorts against the onslaught of depression and suicidality. Here's the truth: God created us in his image, and he felt emotions too. We can see in the Bible instances where God became angry, when he rejoiced, and so much more. Even more profoundly, we can see the same emotional variances in Jesus, who the author of Hebrews tells us is the exact representation of God the Father. We even see where the Holy Spirit can be grieved, an emotion. If all the members of the Trinity feel things, and if we are created in the image of God, then why shouldn't we feel too?

I had a hard time learning this lesson. In my home, emotionality equaled weakness, so I learned to stuff my emotions whenever they came to the surface. I believed that my intellect was the center of my being and that I needed to live out of that part of myself. So, for many years, that's exactly what I did: I pretended that painful things didn't hurt, I stuffed them down into my gut, and I lived out of my brain. Except this didn't work very well. I found my emotions escaping out into my daily life at unexpected and unhelpful moments. I overreacted to small things and even to perceived offenses for no obvious reason. It took this moment with Kevin to help me see that I should give space to my circumstantial emotions because they are valid. When I'm feeling grief or any other emotion, I have to give it space to breathe. I can use my brain to cross-examine my emotions, but I can't pretend they don't exist. I learned that it's not only okay but preferential to allow myself to engage with my emotions. Initially, I found myself embarrassed that I didn't have more help for Kevin, but if I'm honest, I was equally taken aback by his emotionality. I couldn't be equipped to deal with that moment because I hadn't given myself permission to feel as deeply as he was feeling, so I didn't know what to do. I accidentally gave him stellar advice, but it certainly wasn't planned.

In the years since that moment though, I have learned how to give myself permission to sit with my emotions. It's vital to process the circumstances that happen in life, if only to avoid them ruling us later through that unintentional oozing I spoke of earlier. I know now that I usually process things externally, which means I can't sit in silence and process anything. I need some sort of outlet to help me walk through the emotions. Sometimes that means I talk with my wife, Barbara, or someone else safe about what I'm feeling in response to a series of circumstances, instead of letting it simmer in my innards. Sometimes it means I journal about it. Seeing my words on a computer screen helps me to process almost as well as talking to someone, especially if it's a particularly tender moment to work through. If you are an external processor like me, both methods can be invaluable. If you are an internal processor, then you can sit with your emotions and analyze them to understand where you are with them. I admit that I can't offer much advice to internal processors, because I'm just not built that way. I would tell you, though, to make sure you give yourself plenty of space to work through your circumstances because it's not always a quick process.

One last thing worth mentioning: if you are trying to work through some sort of grief, you need to know that grief isn't linear. You won't ever arrive at a moment where you are "done" grieving. An unexpected moment will hit you weirdly, and you will feel all the strength of your grief as if it just happened. It means you still have an emotional connection with the person or event you are grieving, which you should. Over time, these weird little moments will grow less and less common, but the hole in your heart from the loss will never fully dissipate. Don't feel like you're somehow less than because you haven't finished processing your grief. Nobody finishes with grief, ever.

Why It Matters

It's not uncommon for depression or suicidality to take grief as a jumping-off point, to run with the built-up emotions of a troubling time and bring us to unhealthy places. Thankfully, the Bible isn't silent on what to do in grief. There are several times when we see the way that grief impinges on someone's life, but perhaps the most poignant is Job. As you may recall, Job had a series of terrible events befall him in a very short time. He lost his wealth, his children, and his health in just a matter of a few days. It got to the point where even his wife told him to curse God and die. Much in the story of Job would speak to how we could respond to calamities, but I want to focus on what his friends did. Let's pick up the story in Job 2:11–13:

> When three of Job's friends heard of the tragedy he had suffered, they got together and traveled from their homes to comfort and console him. Their names were Eliphaz the Temanite, Bildad the

Shuhite, and Zophar the Naamathite. When they saw Job from a distance, they scarcely recognized him. Wailing loudly, they tore their robes and threw dust into the air over their heads to show their grief. Then they sat on the ground with him for seven days and nights. No one said a word to Job, for they saw that his suffering was too great for words.

The first thing that's worth noting: these three friends traveled to be with Job. There weren't phones, so they did the best they could and got there to just be present with their friend Job as soon as possible. There's powerful commentary here for those of us with mental health conditions, especially considering the call to transparency from the last chapter. Not everyone will have calamities befall them that are as obvious as Job's, where friends will hear of them. No, we usually suffer our mental health conditions in silence, which means nobody will know what we're going through unless we tell them. We might feel unloved or not cared for because others aren't traveling to comfort and console us, but nobody knows what's happening if we don't tell them. It seems unfair, but it's on us to be honest with our friends so they can support us in times of travail. If Kevin hadn't told me his dad had died, I might not have heard until the funeral. But he knew he needed support, so he reached out. We must all do the same, so our circumstances don't entrap us in loneliness.

The next thing that's striking about these verses: Job was unrecognizable physically. The narrative tells us that he had boils from head to toe and scratched at them with a shard of pottery. His friends didn't even know where to find Job until they got closer. This reminds me of the wonderful scene from *Hook* when the Lost Boys don't believe Robin Williams used to be Peter Pan, until one of the boys grabs his face, smushes it about, and forces a ridiculous smile. Then he says, "Oh, there you are, Peter!"[6] I believe it

6. *Hook*, directed by Steven Spielberg (1991, Amblin Entertainment and Tri-Star Pictures).

could have been something similar with Job. Eliphaz, Bildad, and Zophar knew Job's house, but they didn't see anyone who looked like Job on the premises. Still, they drew near and finally recognized him underneath the mess of his physical appearance. It's vital to note that Job didn't shrink away from his friends because of his appearance, and we can learn from this too. We might be emotionally distorted or even physically unkempt because of grief or depression, but we must not hide when others come looking for us. We might be nearly unrecognizable like Job, but our true friends will find us anyway. We have to let them do just that.

The last and perhaps most important thing: Eliphaz, Bildad, and Zophar joined in Job's grief. For a full week, they sat on the ground in the ashes with him, said nothing, and wept with him. Things got dicey once these friends started opening their mouths because they began to question whether Job brought his problems upon himself, but for that first week, they remained the best possible friends. When we grieve or are in a season of significant mental turmoil, we need others who will just enter into grief with us, no questions asked. That's why my statement to Kevin ended up being so profound to him. I recognized and entered into his grief. We have to allow others to enter our grief and our mental health challenges with us. Otherwise, we miss out on the community that God intends for us to have throughout the dark seasons.

How It Applies

1. Have you ever lost someone close to you, and how would you describe the emotions of those moments? If you haven't, think about another time that you've grieved something and reflect on your emotions from that moment.

2. If you've been in seasons of grief, what were some of the most helpful things that others said to you during that time? What made them helpful?

Resilient and Redeemed

3. Have you ever felt like you've been taught that emotion should be managed and stuffed down because you're a Christian? If so, how did you respond to that teaching?

4. When did you last let someone just sit with you, say nothing, and grieve alongside you? How did that make you feel as a friend and as a human being?

5. What do you think about the idea that God wants us to be in community while grieving, and what might that look like in your life?

What God Thinks

Be happy with those who are happy, and weep with those who weep.

Romans 12:15

Weeping with those who weep is a command in the New Testament, which seems pretty amazing when you think of the complexities of entering someone else's pain and feeling it with them. But that's what the apostle Paul tells us to do. Maybe you've been on the other side of this experience, where somebody has wept with you while you've been in despair. Or perhaps you've always been on the outside looking in, wondering where your true friends are and why nobody stands in the gap for you in your pain. Either way, the command of God says to weep with those who weep. Let's flip the script a little as we end this chapter and think about how and who we can weep with. Who needs support in your life because of a rough time? What would it look like to weep with them? Maybe that's as simple as a text message, checking in on an old friend. Perhaps it means taking that old friend out for some coffee to see what's up in their life. Prayerfully consider how you can be that weeping, invested friend for someone who might need it today.

58

5

The Superman Cape

Be on guard. Stand firm in the faith. Be courageous. Be strong. And do everything with love.

1 Corinthians 16:13–14

My Story

A large box came in the mail one day. It wasn't from Amazon or one of the other online retailers and I wasn't expecting anything, so I had no idea what to expect. I don't remember what I hoped it would be when I opened this mystery box from a mystery sender with my name on it, but I know this—I didn't expect a Superman cape. But that's what I got, an extra-long Superman cape, just the right size for extra-tall Chris. I'll admit it, I found myself very confused by this mystery gift. It didn't make any sense at all, and I nearly threw out the whole thing. Then I saw the note, and everything shifted for me. At the bottom of the box, I found a handwritten note from my friend Bria: "Chris, I know you feel like you can't do anything right today, and it's been that way for a while now. But you're wrong. Not only are you doing the right things, but you can also do anything you put your mind to. You are a superhero. You just needed your cape." It might seem cheesy to you, and honestly, on most days it would probably seem cheesy to me too, but on that day it just hit right. I started crying.

My wife walked into the room and found herself thoroughly confused because she saw me wiping my tears away with a random Superman cape. You gotta love married life, right? Barbara walked over to me and rubbed my back, then gently asked about the cape and the tears. I showed her the note from Bria, and she replied as only my wife could: "I've been trying to tell you this for years." She wasn't wrong, but for some reason, the Superman cape made it real for me.

The past few months had been incredibly rough for me. I experienced a lot of failure in my parenting journey as my kids grew older and made foolish decisions that I felt responsible for. I had hit a solid brick wall in my writing. I had hoped to find an agent for a particular book, but instead I received about seventy-five rejection letters. I struggled to find a place or a way to lead in our new church, so I felt largely useless in that regard. I struggled in my work life for reasons I won't go into here (they're boring, trust me). My wife and I found ourselves on the rocks a bit because I internalized all this failure, real and perceived. In short, my depression rose again because I felt useless in most areas of my life. I just felt as though I couldn't measure up to my own standards. Worse yet, I felt like I disappointed other people too—my boss, my wife, my sons and daughter, my church, and even God.

So, my friend sent this Superman cape into a whirlwind of despair and disappointment. It hit home for me. Somehow, such an unexpected and surprising gift jumped over all my defenses, and I received the words of encouragement she wrote to me as gospel truth. I had been a superhero without a cape, but now thanks to Bria I had my cape. This bizarre little gift stayed hanging in a prominent place in my bedroom for about eight years. I'll be honest with you and tell you something I'm a little embarrassed to admit: most weeks, I looked at that cape and remembered those words from Bria and took courage from them. This simple gift made a real difference in my life. It stood as tangible evidence that God wasn't done with me even though I found myself in a rough season. It became proof that I wasn't useless. It was precisely what I needed to get through a very difficult season.

A few years ago, I had a close friend going through an incredibly difficult time of her own, surrounded by failure and disappointment that left her wondering if God still liked or loved her anymore. I had the privilege of sending her my Superman cape then. In a handwritten note, I shared how Bria had sent this cape to me when I needed it. I shared how it became a daily reminder of the goodness of God in my life, of the fact that I was a superhero who just needed a cape. And I told her that now she needed this supersized Superman cape. She had lost her cape, but I would help her by giving her mine. You see, I didn't need my cape anymore since its lessons had been ingrained in my mind and heart, so I could share it with her.

What I Learned

So, what did I learn from the Superman cape, you might ask? That's a fair question. I hinted at some of the lessons above, but there's so much more to unpack. The biggest thing the Superman cape taught me is that I'm never defined by my present circumstances. It's far too easy to fall into the trap of thinking that whatever my last few days look like describes me perfectly. This leads to a dangerous pattern of severe highs and supreme lows, often following quickly one after another. I had not yet learned to center myself outside my circumstances, so I allowed the things that happened to me to determine how I thought about myself. This resulted in incredible emotional instability and left those around me confused by my reactions. I couldn't maintain a sense of purpose or identity that existed outside of my moments.

This feels like an easy thing to fix, but when situations pile up in rapid succession as they did in my life, it's not so simple. It's far too easy to fall into the trap of either believing your own hype or believing the worst about yourself. We find ourselves struggling to find centeredness because things are just happening too fast, so we instead react to the circumstances. This produces inconsistency and internal confusion that's hard to overcome without help from somewhere or someone else. That's what the cape and the accompanying note provided me—a reminder that my experiences don't define me. I looked at the cape and reminded myself that I'm a free moral agent in my own life. I wasn't forced to do anything or act a certain way by anyone. No, I had the capability to choose how I wanted to act, even if circumstances seemed to be conspiring against me. By hanging the cape in my room, I had a visible reminder that I could *choose* what I did in my life. Even if the results weren't what I hoped for or expected, I could make choices to influence my future and the lives of those I cared for.

But the cape did more than that. It began to show me the role that self-discipline plays in the Christian life. If we're not careful, we can start to believe this subtle little lie that says everything good that happens in our lives happens because God accomplishes it directly, as though we have no part to play in the event. While there are certainly moments where God does a miraculous thing without any involvement from us—like bringing us to faith in Jesus—many times we do have a role in how things happen. I was reminded of the role of self-discipline, that I have to be an active participant in my own life. I was reminded of times when the apostle Paul talked about running in such a way as to win or beating his body into submission for Christ (see 1 Corinthians 9:24–27). These are choices that he made to further his intimacy with Jesus, and I had to learn to do the same thing.

I began to consciously consider questions like this: What does it mean *today* to redeem my time for God? What is it about *this* circumstance that God could be using to draw me closer to him? How can I manage my emotions *right now* and better remember that God calls me to live out the fruits of the Spirit each day? What are the habits or relationships that are holding me back from running my race in such a way as to win? As I grappled with these questions and others like them, I learned how to function in a more self-disciplined way in my life. I began to see baby fruit that I hadn't experienced before, like emotional stability. I still had a long way to go before these fruits would be full-size, but this was the beginning of a very important journey for me.

The cape also gave me hope in a very specific way. Before this unexpected gift, I started to feel like I might be destined for failure after failure because I didn't understand the rules of life or something like that. I wondered if I couldn't trust my intuition or if my gut had been busted, and if I needed to lean fully on other people for good decisions. This cape stood as a reminder to me that I had seen some bad luck, but that I wasn't the personification of bad luck because there's no such thing as bad luck personified. Instead, I found myself in a rough season that I needed to weather, and things would eventually look up again. So, the Superman cape reminded me that things would definitely improve. The cape showed me that life has its ups and downs, but neither defines my personhood. I found the courage to trust myself again with decisions, instead of shrinking back in fear or worry.

I battled against the depression that crept back into the forefront of my psyche because my friend reminded me that I could accomplish great things. I borrowed strength from Bria through the cape she sent me to battle these thoughts of negativity and push forward with a better attitude toward life in general. Instead of assuming everything would fall apart, I hypothesized that things could potentially turn out for the better too.

There's a funny side story related to capes that I have to share with you because it's one of the things I learned from this incident in my life. In case you haven't figured it out by now, pessimism

Life has its ups and downs, but neither defines my personhood.

could be called my unfortunate calling card. My wife sees the glass half full, and sometimes her cheery disposition irritates me. I once told her in frustration that if she ever became a superhero, she would be Silver Lining Girl because she can find goodness in even the worst of circumstances. As a coded reference to that conversation, we agreed that if I felt her cheerfulness starting to irritate me, I could ask her to take her cape off. This would be a way to communicate what I felt without starting a fight and would give her a chance to reset her approach to me in a given situation. So, once I stopped crying about the cape, my wife and I had a good laugh that she might be Silver Lining Girl, but I had a cape. This moment reminded me that God most definitely has a sense of humor, and he will use even the most insider of inside jokes to communicate something to us. God told me in the subtlest of ways that I could use a little more Silver Lining Girl in my own life.

Why It Matters

When we allow moments in our lives to define our emotionality, we are setting ourselves up for a tumultuous season. God doesn't call us to live in tumult though; he calls us to live in victory. Romans 8:37 says it most plainly: "No, despite all these things, overwhelming victory is ours through Christ, who loved us." You might ask about the context of the verse because it says, "all these things," and that's a great question. There's a laundry list of exactly the types of things that make us feel like we aren't superheroes: trouble, calamity, persecution, hunger, destitution, danger, and death threats. The apostle Paul had experienced all of these firsthand, so he wasn't talking hypothetically. No, he spoke from hard-won, tested faith that went through hell and came out victorious on the other side. He survived a stoning and more than one riot and having people from another city start trouble because they heard he came to town. Paul understood how hard life can be, yet he penned these words.

Sometimes the phrase *the victorious Christian life* is code for living as though the circumstances in life can't hurt you, even though we know they can. In these circles, being an overcomer might look like pretending that there's nothing wrong when you don't have enough money in your bank account for both food and rent, but that's not what Paul means here. The type of faith he's talking about recognizes the pain that can come from this life and still chooses to step into victory because of the love of God in our lives. Jesus modeled this lifestyle. He's the one who chose to give his life as a ransom for us all on the cross and trusted God would resurrect him in vindication.

Another meaningful thought in this context can be found in 2 Timothy 1:7, which says, "For God has not given us a spirit of fear and timidity, but of power, love, and self-discipline." Let's focus on the first part of that verse for now. How often do we engage our life out of a place of fear or timidity? How easily do we assume the worst, take a passive stance, and wait for life to happen? I had started to do this before my Superman cape came to me. I believed I couldn't change anything, so why even bother trying? I had lain down on the job of life, so to speak. I gave up before any decisions even came my way because I didn't believe I could offer anything useful to anyone at all. But this is accepting defeat before the proverbial game even starts. And for that reason, I know it's not the heart of God for us.

No, God calls us to live with power, love, and self-discipline. Each of these adds color to the conversation. Power is what we grab hold of when we let go of passivity. Power says we believe our choices matter and we can make a difference in this world. Power won't settle for anything less than a fully engaged life. Love pushes us to think beyond ourselves because sometimes (not always) depression comes as a self-serving series of thoughts. When we're burdened with depressive ideas, we aren't easily able to think of anyone else because we're focused on ourselves. We can't find the emotional strength to push past our own insecurities and fears to think of others, but love paves the path forward. When we fixate on love, we will find the courage and ability to consider how our actions impact others instead of only ourselves.

We've been talking about self-discipline for this entire chapter. It allows us to find a center outside ourselves and not be swayed by the circumstances of our lives. Self-discipline means we properly weigh events in light of our view of ourselves and our responsibilities. Self-discipline strengthens us to power through hard times. But heed a word of caution here about powering through hard times. Sometimes, self-discipline can be a menace in our lives if we aren't careful. Sometimes, we need to slow down, power down, and rest to fight another day. The answer isn't always to try harder, as a lifetime of trying harder can lead to burnout and frustration.

I want to take a moment to remind you about the resilience course that I've created especially for the readers of this book. You can find the QR code for this course in the *Additional Resources* section at the back of the book. Resilience and the ups and downs of life are more closely related than we might imagine at first, and this is one topic I address in this course.

How It Applies

1. When did you last receive a surprising gift that ministered to your soul in an unexpected way? Would you consider giving a gift like this to someone important in your life, and what might that look like?
2. How much do you struggle not to allow yourself, your capabilities, and your strength to be defined by your present circumstances?
3. Do you find it hard to trust your intuition or your gut in difficult circumstances? Why or why not?
4. How often do you feel like you live in overwhelming victory like the apostle Paul talked about in Romans 8:37? What keeps you from living there more often?

5. Between power, love, and self-discipline, which do you struggle with the most? Why do you think that might be the case?

What God Thinks

No, despite all these things, overwhelming victory is ours through Christ, who loved us.

Romans 8:37

You might read that verse and scoff. "Yeah, right. I've never had more than a few moments of overwhelming victory." But the Bible calls us to this. Don't hear this as judgment, but as an opportunity. What if—just hear me out—what if God really calls us to have overwhelming victory despite those moments when everything falls apart? What would that look like, and how might we get there? I know we aren't going to solve this problem with a few words, so I'm not even going to try, but I do want to challenge you to raise your expectation level just a bit. This promise wouldn't be in the Bible if it weren't true, even if it's not something you're experiencing in your life. Here's the simple challenge for you. Pray a prayer that sounds something like this:

God, I am not experiencing overwhelming victory. I don't even expect it or know what that might look like. But I believe your Bible to be true. Grant me faith to begin to look for this type of victory in my life. I want to believe this as truth, even though it's not been my experience. Amen.

Now, let's wait and see how God answers that prayer.

67

6

My Weird Counselors

He [God] sends rain on the just and the unjust alike.
Matthew 5:45

My Story

I knew I needed to take my mental health more seriously. My depression and suicidality visited me more often now, and I needed to take steps to get them under control. I still took medication to remove the edge from the dark seasons I experienced, but the dark seasons kept piling up. I needed more support to make a dent in the darkness. I had been reluctant to find a counselor for a very practical reason. I didn't really know where to start because there are so many counselors with so many different specialties and training and backgrounds. It felt like I would be throwing a dart at a balloon in a dark room, hoping that I might at least be facing the right direction. How likely would I be to hit that balloon and end up with a solid counselor? I thought the odds poor, so I did nothing for a long time. Finally, at the end of one of my arguments with my wife during a depressive episode, she told me

I needed to find a counselor. She said that she couldn't be the only one trying to help me navigate my mental health. I needed to pull my own weight.

For some reason, this time the conversation stuck in my head. I say "this time" because Barbara had certainly told me this before, but I never took her seriously. At any rate, I understood that I needed to change the way I operated, so I started searching. I didn't know any better, so I went to my insurance's website and looked for counselors included in our coverage. I found one that sounded like she might be helpful, though in truth I largely guessed about what *helpful* might mean, and I scheduled an appointment for a few weeks out.

I can't put words to how nervous and anxious I felt about this appointment. Part of me felt convinced I had to be a failure for even needing a counselor in the first place, and I found it difficult to shake that feeling. Beyond the sense of failure though, I felt the same type of nervousness I used to feel before a job interview or a first date (though I barely remember first-date jitters, if I'm being honest—I've been married a long time, folks). What if my new counselor told me that I wasn't really battling depression, but something else altogether? What if she said I should be able to handle myself without the extra support of a counselor? What if she attacked me instead of trying to help me? I had a whir of emotions going through my mind, largely fear based on lack of knowledge. I'd never gone to a counselor before.

I never considered approaching the first session almost as an interview with the counselor, trying to gauge if she would be a good fit for me. I now have this approach, and I highly recommend it. After all, we are trusting this person with a lot of our frustrations, anxieties, and dark moments. Even in the best of circumstances, it will take time to develop trust with a counselor, so it only makes sense to start cautiously.

I didn't approach things this way with my first counselor. She asked why I scheduled my appointment, and I laid it all out for her.

I told her that I had battled depression and suicidality my entire life and as a result had a lot of conflict in my marriage too. And I didn't just end there as an introduction. I probably talked for fifteen minutes straight about all my problems and how I needed help. I didn't know how to read the room, so I didn't understand that I went too fast. To her credit, she didn't just usher me out of her office when I laid all of that on her. Instead, she explained the types of counseling that she did and how she thought she'd be able to help me.

Despite my jumping into the deep end with our first appointment, things progressed nicely after a few meetings. She had given me some ways to reframe my thoughts when I felt the negativity piling up on me, and she had even given me some suggestions on how to lighten the load for my wife. Then the wheels fell off. I haven't mentioned this yet in this book, but I have a seizure disorder where I freeze or zone out for fifteen to sixty seconds a few times on most days. I had one of my seizures in the middle of one of our appointments while I talked. So, here's how this looked to my counselor: I froze mid-sentence for about a minute, then kept talking as if nothing had happened (because I'm not always aware of my seizures). This time though, I did read the room, mostly because she had a look of abject horror on her face. I asked her if I'd had a seizure, and she stammered, "I guess so. I don't know what to do here." I suggested that she go get my wife from the waiting room, and together my wife and I counseled my counselor. Despite our reassurances, she never dropped that look of horror from her face. I awkwardly ended my appointment about ten minutes early and never went back.

After a brief hiatus, I found another counselor. This time, I went a bit more slowly and didn't dump all my problems on her in the first appointment. I did lay out that I have an ongoing struggle with depression and suicidality and that I needed additional strategies and support for my battles. Pleased with how things progressed in the beginning, I opened up about some of the specific aspects of my depression. One time, I mentioned in passing that I had a hard time reconciling my foundational belief in a good God with the darkness that remained part of my daily life. She thought this gave her a green light to rail on organized religion. For the next twenty-five minutes of my appointment, she aggressively attacked all faiths, but specifically Christianity. She mentioned that all versions of God are nothing but a crutch for the weak-willed and encouraged me to let go of my crutch and walk under my own power because I didn't need the falsehood of faith.

I debriefed with my wife after this diatribe on my faith, trying to figure out how to respond to it in a meaningful way that remained true to my core beliefs. Eventually, I decided to end my care with this counselor, but I needed to provide an explanation to her in this case. I penned a letter where I explained that she had offended me with her attack on Christianity. I had never invited her to critique my faith or tell me to leave my faith in the dust. I didn't appreciate the liberties she took to share her opinions with me after I simply shared another element of the struggles I had at that time. I didn't expect to hear back from this counselor, and I didn't. Part of me wonders if the office staff even shared the letter with her, but regardless, I knew I had shared my heart about her misstep and I felt satisfied.

What I Learned

After these two mishaps with counselors, I decided to take a break from finding another therapist to help me. I wasn't convinced that I would find one who would be fruitful for me, so I decided I would use the tools they had given me and go it alone again. This was a mistake, one that I would regret over the next several years, but I look back on this decision and see why I made it. I had been hurt in two very different, very specific ways by counselors. It didn't feel worth risking it again with another stranger.

When I eventually went back to finding a therapist, I armed myself with the right types of questions to ask during the feeling-out period, based on the ways my previous counselors disregarded me. My first counselor wasn't equipped to deal with the medical side of my reality and essentially flipped her lid when I had a seizure. My seizures aren't likely to go away (they haven't yet anyway), so the possibility of having a seizure while in a counseling session remains. My therapist needs to be able to manage this reasonably well, even if it means letting me take the lead after a seizure. I don't typically hurt myself, so it's just a matter of reorienting me back to reality after a seizure. Now I know I need to explain that I have a seizure disorder that doesn't physically harm me, and check with my therapist to make sure they are amenable to reorienting me.

My second counselor disparaged my faith, a central part of my life. I simply can't have a counselor who is quick to disregard the role of faith in a person's life. Now I don't want you to hear me saying that you should only use Christian counselors. As a matter of fact, my current counselor has a history as a Catholic priest and now leans slightly into Buddhist teachings, so I don't even have a strictly Christian therapist. We will spend more time talking about how I found my current counselor in a later chapter, but for now, I want to emphasize that I need to have someone who isn't going to downplay or speak against my faith if I'm expressing struggles with it. So, this becomes another question that I must ask any current or future therapist—whether they will leave space for my faith to coexist with my struggles without engaging in negative reactions themselves. Your questions for your potential therapists will grow out of your own experiences, values, health conditions, and heart. These questions will grow out of the answer to one core inquiry: what will allow you to trust someone enough to open up to them so that they can provide you with useful guidance? A counselor without trust isn't useful to anyone and wastes your time and money.

Why It Matters

The key takeaway from these vignettes in my own experiences with counselors, something that took me a long time to learn, is that my healing journey should be treated as something precious and tender because God loves me deeply. God remains intimately interested in seeing me (and you) become whole and healthy, and everyone involved should be in agreement with God. Our Creator isn't up in the heavens laughing at our brokenness or aggravated that we aren't further along in our path toward wholeness. No, the imagery painted in Scripture looks very different indeed. Perhaps the best verse to help us understand how God views our challenges is Psalm 56:8—"You keep track of all my sorrows. You have collected all my tears in your bottle. You have recorded each one in your book."

Often in our sadness and tearful moments, we accuse God of being distant because we don't always feel his presence in our lives. Yet this Scripture gives us a completely different picture. Here we see a God deeply invested in our sorrows. He is actively involved in our sadness and participates alongside us in our sorrows. He collects our tears and records our sorrows in a book. God knows what we are going through, he pays attention, and he longs to see us free from these moments. When we trust someone to walk alongside us in our healing, they should be treating us with the same tenderness as God. Now, clearly nobody will rise to the level of God's perfect love for us, but their posture should be one of caring and tender concern.

Let me say something else here too, for those of you who need to hear this. Seeking out a counselor or therapist to see you through a tough season or longer shouldn't be seen as problematic. There are Christian leaders out there who say that all we need to find our full healing is the Bible and some spiritual disciplines. I one-hundred-percent disagree. I believe this approach can end up being very harmful. We need the full resources available to us to

> *Seeking out a counselor or therapist to see you through a tough season or longer shouldn't be seen as problematic. There are Christian leaders out there who say that all we need to find our full healing is the Bible and some spiritual disciplines. I one-hundred-percent disagree.*

find health. Yes, the Bible as the written counsel of God becomes a grand resource, and yes, prayer soothes our souls, but it's not uncommon for both to not be enough. Think of my story with my first pastor. I did all the right things, and it didn't matter—depression won battles in my mind. I needed medication and a good counselor and a support team and daily habits to help me find my center and begin to reestablish healthy patterns in my life. You might need the same, and there's no shame in that. Matthew 5 says that God causes rain to fall on the just and the unjust. This means that common graces are available to everyone regardless of spiritual positioning before God. Medication, therapy, mindfulness, daily habits, and supportive friends are all common graces. Let's take advantage of everything available to us to find our healing, okay?

Let's dwell for a moment longer on how God views us when we are busted and broken and trying to find the human help we need to get better. It's easy to feel as though God might be disappointed that we aren't farther along or more mature, or that God has gone on ahead of us and waits impatiently for us to catch up to him somewhere down the path. John 14:18 stands in direct opposition to this idea; Jesus promises us, "No, I will not abandon you as orphans—I will come to you." It's easy to feel like an orphan when times are tough, but this direct promise from our Savior says he will not leave us without support or parental love. And the beautiful thing about this promise: Jesus is talking about the gift of the Holy Spirit. We can read elsewhere in the Bible that God gives us the Holy Spirit when we confess Jesus as our Savior. The Holy Spirit who dwells within us because we are followers of Christ proves that God stands undoubtedly for us.

I made a mistake in the selection of my first two counselors. I didn't honor my own journey enough to recognize that others should be as invested as God in my healing. Neither supported my growth toward wholeness, and this broke the heart of God. In an ironic turn of events, the very people I chose to help me walk through my pain ended up causing more pain and creating more barriers to my healing instead of facilitating it. Armed with a proper understanding of God's heart for me and how he views my pain, I'm now equipped to be much more careful and discerning with my therapists.

How It Applies

1. If you have sought a therapist, what made you decide to start looking for one? If you haven't, what keeps you from looking for one?

2. If you have gone to a counselor, how did you select your first counselor? How overwhelmed did you become in the process of trying to find the right one?

3. Have you ever had a "weird counselor" or one who was just a bad fit for you? Describe that experience. How easily did you recover from it?

4. Do you have extra circumstances like medical conditions that your therapists might need to be made aware of as you test out if they can be a good fit for you?

5. When you feel like God has abandoned you and left you as an orphan, or that he doesn't care about your pain, how do you counteract these thoughts?

What God Thinks

No, I will not abandon you as orphans—I will come to you.

John 14:18

There are times when the medical world will seem to abandon us, and it will be tempting to believe that God has done the same thing. Yet this promise stands against that temptation because Jesus spoke these words directly to his disciples and consequently to us. Jesus says he will never abandon us. We will never be orphans. A testimony of God's tenderness and goodness in our lives always remains, even in the darkest moments. That's the challenge though—to find those testimonies. Let's practice that right now, just to get accustomed to the idea of actively looking for God's presence in our dark seasons. The best way to see the testimony of God in our lives might be to ask him to show us, because we often lack his perspective in a situation. So, join me in this simple prayer as you reconsider a dark season in your life:

God, I can't find you in this moment of my life. I believe your Bible, but it seems like you were nowhere to be found. Show me where you were. I want to understand how you collected my tears in a bottle, because from where I sit, you weren't near me. O God, prove me wrong.

By the way, God is perfectly okay with this type of aggressive prayer, so don't hesitate to pray in this way. God welcomes our testing of his goodness, and he's up to the challenge. After praying this, sit in silence for at least ninety seconds and listen carefully for the whisper of God's presence or unexpected thoughts (often the Holy Spirit speaks in this way).

7

How Gritty Friendships Saved My Life

Don't just pretend to love others. Really love them.
Romans 12:9

My Story

The day I almost ended my life started out just like most other days. I ushered the kids out the door to school and got to work. Nothing out of the ordinary happened, and it stayed that way until around eleven that morning. Then, seemingly from nowhere, I found myself bowled over by a wave of depressive thoughts. Don't get me wrong, I hadn't been in a good spot emotionally for months, but this felt different.

My thoughts weren't my normal depression thoughts. No, these thoughts came at me very specific and pointed. *You're never going to overcome this sadness, Chris. It's not going to pass. You are going to be in this pain for the rest of your life, and you can't bear*

79

that. You should take those pills and end it now. I couldn't shake that last thought. *Take those pills and end it now.*

I'd been suicidal before, but never with a plan, not since my teenage years anyway. And here's the thing: I didn't really want to die. I just wanted the pain to end, and these thoughts convinced me that the pain wouldn't end any other way.

I sat with these thoughts for a while, then I went to get the pills. I looked at the pills I wanted to take for a few minutes, weighing the possibilities. *What would my kids think if I died by suicide? How would this impact my wife? Would everyone really be better off without me? Would my family be scarred if they found me? Would it still be worth it to end the pain?*

I determined that I would call my wife at work and decide what to do based on how she responded. I wasn't sure at that point if she would even put up an argument because I'd been such an emotional mess the last few months. I went back and forth on whether I should even call her for a few minutes. I didn't want to bother her at work; she had a high-stress job at the time. Then I had to decide how to tell her. Should I act like everything was okay and then drop a bombshell on her, or just cut to the chase? I chose the latter.

When my wife picked up the phone, I told her I wanted to die by suicide using pills. She took a deep breath and asked for a moment to gather her thoughts. "I wasn't expecting this," she said. My wife worked as a nurse at a children's cancer center, so she didn't work the type of job where she could just drop everything and come home. Even if she could come home, it would take forty-five minutes, and that could be too long.

The decisions she made next are the reason I'm still here today. "Chris, I *can't* leave work today. I have a couple of high acuity patients and there's nobody to take care of them if I come home. But I'm going to marshal the troops and get you taken care of. Hang with me on the phone for a few minutes." I mumbled something and stayed on the phone, and then I started getting text messages.

A lot of text messages. I asked Barbara if I could let her go so I could answer the texts. "Are you going to stay with me?" she asked. "Yes, I just want to answer these texts."

I had two texts from my friends Tim and Kevin. Both asked why my day became so rough and how they could help. I told them both that I felt suicidal and wasn't sure I could make it through the day. As soon as I sent that message to Kevin and he read it, I got a phone call from him.

"Hey, buddy, don't you give up on us. We need you here in this life. I don't know what I'd do without your friendship, Chris." I heard Kevin's words, and they lifted me up a little bit. I murmured something resembling a thank you. We talked for a few more minutes as he encouraged me to keep moving forward.

While we talked, Tim texted me again. He told me that as his best friend, he needed me to keep going. Life wouldn't be the same without me in it, he said. He needed me to stick around because my friendship mattered deeply to him. He wanted me to stick through this difficult time because he and his wife loved me and didn't want to miss me because I died.

I started to move away from the pills, then I got another call from my friend Lindsay. My wife really had marshaled the troops. "How are you hanging in there, Chris?" she asked. I confessed, "Pretty badly. I'm suicidal right now." She gently talked to me for about ten minutes, telling me that the world improved with me in it. Lindsay spoke of times I had been her best support through some of her specific challenges, and how she knew those times would come again. "I need you to stay around, Chris."

Despite everything my friends said, I couldn't let go of this idea. I needed to get away from the pain. I didn't want to tell them this because I felt so much shame. *I'm a Christian—this shouldn't be happening to me.* But this is where I found myself, and it seemed that I couldn't escape it.

I let Lindsay go because my friend Joel called. This conversation had a different feel to it. Joel questioned me in more detailed and more direct ways because he works as a chaplain at a mental health facility, so he was assessing me as we spoke. Joel asked me if I had a plan. He asked if I thought myself ready to execute the plan, and I admitted I still stood in front of the pills, trying to decide my next step. Joel told me I was a danger to myself and that he would get me the help I needed. He told me he would drive to my house, that we would stay on the phone until he got there, and then we would discuss the next steps.

Ten minutes of talking later, Joel arrived at my house. He told me that he would help me admit myself to a psychiatric hospital. I wasn't happy, but I did as he asked. I packed a bag of clothes and books, the whole time arguing with him. It's almost funny in retrospect—I found myself both compliant and angry at the same time. I argued with him as I packed my bag, telling him I didn't have any problems while I still thought about those pills in the other room. A few minutes later we got in his car and left for the hospital.

With Joel's help, I admitted myself to the psych ward and stayed a week. The doctors and staff worked with me to adjust my medications to help me find some emotional and mental steadiness. We had some good conversations about how to find and keep that stability. I learned a lot about myself and my mental health in the mental health hospital. It would be an exaggeration to tell you that this ended my suicidal thoughts, but it guided me in the right direction. As you'll see in later chapters, this wouldn't be my last tango with suicidality, though.

What I Learned

As I consider this moment in my life, gratitude wells up in my soul for my wife and all my friends. Everyone showed up when I needed them the most. I'm still here, I know I'm loved, and I know I'm not too much for my friends. They didn't hide behind not knowing what to say or being uncomfortable or thinking good Christians don't struggle with suicide. They just showed up. And now I can show up for them and others today because nobody left me alone on that day. Nobody had answers for me, but they showed up nevertheless, and their presence changed my life for the better. I literally may not have made it to today if not for my friends' kindness, their goodness, and their defiant care for me when I didn't care about myself. Their earthy, gritty, grinding-it-out-in-the-grime-of-life friendships saved my life that day.

So often in my own life, I feel like I have to supply answers to my friends to be valuable to them. This experience shows me that presence can be at least as powerful as having answers. I had four friends stand in the gap for me when I didn't have the ability to think clearly for myself. Three of them simply told me that they loved and valued me, and one used his skill as a mental health professional to help me get to someplace safe.

If Barbara hadn't marshaled the troops for me, I might not be here today to tell this story of my suicidal moment. Kevin, Tim, and Lindsay reminded me that I'm valuable and worthwhile, not just as a human being but as their friend. This became the very beginning of my recovery from my suicidal ideations at that moment, though it would take much longer for me to fully recover stability. Joel came with his understanding of how to work with mental health patients and supplied the expertise necessary to make sure I didn't make a decision I would regret. Joel came wearing two hats though—one as a mental health professional and one as a friend—because he couldn't ignore a decade of friendship. I've had the opportunity recently to offer my presence and support to other friends who found themselves in crisis, and thinking back on this moment in my life has given me the liberty to know that I don't need to have all the answers. Providing a kind heart, a listening ear, and some thoughtful reflection on someone's inherent worth as a human and their personal value to me as a friend offers more than pat answers.

Why It Matters

We are so convinced that life should be a solo sport, and it's a dangerous presumption that gets us into so much trouble. There's a lie in today's culture that says we need to manage all our own stuff without help from others. This lie becomes not only unbiblical but dangerous, especially when we have a mental health crisis. We feel as though we have to handle it on our own terms, but this isn't God's best for us. The New Testament especially overflows with the idea of living a communal, interdependent life with other believers. Hebrews 10:25 tells us, "Let us not neglect our meeting together . . . but encourage one another." This verse speaks about more than showing up to church regularly, though that might be a good start. In this verse, the contrast to not meeting together is to encourage one another. In the context of mental health, this looks exactly like what my friends did when I contemplated suicide. They took time out of their busy days to text and call me, to tell me that I mattered to them, because I needed to hear it at that moment. We've already talked some about transparency in this book, but it's worth revisiting. Others can't sow seeds of meaning and kindness into our lives if we aren't transparent about what we're going through.

Ecclesiastes 4:12 shines more light on the idea of connecting with others to gain strength and consistency in our lives: "A person standing alone can be attacked and defeated, but two can stand back-to-back and conquer. Three are even better, for a triple-braided cord is not easily broken." What a powerful verse on the benefits of community. Too often we live our lives standing alone, so we find ourselves more easily attacked and defeated. Perhaps the attack comes from behind when we least expect it, after we've

> *Others can't sow seeds of meaning and kindness into our lives if we aren't transparent about what we're going through.*

let our guard down. I've been there, when my depression raises its ugly head seemingly out of nowhere and I find myself unprepared for the battle. I know I'm not alone in this.

The verse goes on to say that two can conquer because of an increase in vision. What an enlightening thought about relationships of transparency. We don't always see everything rightly in our lives, but we can lean into relationships of trust to help us understand what we're missing. This will enable us to fight the enemies of our soul, whether self-imposed or external, with greater accuracy and more success. Then Solomon goes on to say that not only are two better than one, but three are better than two. In other words, the more the merrier. Let's not stop at one trusting relationship—the more of these we have, the better equipped we will be for the trials that will inevitably come into our lives. I've never tried to break a triple-braided cord, but it makes sense that this would be much more difficult to snap than a single strand. Let's invest in our own well-being by finding and developing those friendships that will become prepared for war and eventually battle-tested as they help protect us from undue harm.

Friendships are a form of resilience, one that is often overlooked. For a closer examination of resilience, I have created a video course specifically for readers of this book. You can find the QR code for the course in the *Additional Resources* section of the book.

How It Applies

1. Think back on one of your truly low points. How did you get through it? Were other people involved in helping you?
2. How many people do you have in your life who would go to war with you, standing back-to-back and fighting the enemies that come against you?
3. What keeps you from being more transparent with people about your mental health struggles?

4. Have you ever experienced the power of presence in a tough time? What did that look like?

5. What would need to change in your life to have a triple-braided cord of support? What can the first step toward that be, one that you can take today?

What God Thinks

A person standing alone can be attacked and defeated, but two can stand back-to-back and conquer. Three are even better, for a triple-braided cord is not easily broken.

Ecclesiastes 4:12

Maybe you're sitting here reading this verse again and have nothing but frustration boiling up in your gut because you don't have a triple-braided cord and you don't know how to start forming one. You don't want to be on the outside looking in at deep relationships, but you're mostly alone in your life. Take courage, friend—there is hope for you! There's no single, universal step that everyone can take that will promise deep and lasting friendships, but I know this: God's intent isn't for us to be alone. The goal for all of us should be a triple-braided cord, or maybe even more than that, so that we can overcome the battles that will inevitably come. Since we can be certain that God's heart longs for us to be in community, let's take some time now to consider with the Holy Spirit who might be able to join us in our fights. Think about the following questions:

- Who do you know now that you've always wanted to be better friends with?
- Who seems approachable but you've always stayed away from for one reason or another?
- Who has told you in the past they are praying for you, and you actually believed them?

- Who pops into your mind as you think about developing better friendships with others?
- Who do you admire and want to know better?

Consider your answers to the questions above and prayerfully consider reaching out to one of these people who you think you could have a deeper friendship with. Don't jump into the deep end and share your darkest secrets right after you ask if they want to grab a coffee sometime, but be on the lookout for chances to risk deeper relationships. If we don't make different choices, then nothing changes. Let's take those scary first steps of risking transparency with others.

8

Just a Normie

You must grow in the grace and knowledge of our Lord and Savior Jesus Christ.

2 Peter 3:18

My Story

If you're anything like me, your first question upon opening this chapter might be, What exactly is a *normie?* Several other patients called me a normie during my first psych ward visit, and it took me a while to figure out what they meant. I had to ask one of my fellow patients what he meant when he called me a normie. He said, "Chris, you seem like a normal person who has had a tough season, not someone who belongs in this place long-term. You're normal. We're all messed up, but not like you. You can exist on the outside without any major changes in your life. We can't do that." I argued with him, telling him that I clearly couldn't function on the outside or I wouldn't be in the psych ward in the first place, but he continued. "You had a bad moment. We've had a bad life. There's a difference, and you just don't understand."

I pondered this throughout my stay in the mental health ward. Was there truly a difference between me and the other patients? I concluded that the similarities outweighed the differences. I might have come in with nicer clothes or books to read, and I came from a house instead of being homeless, but none of these things changed the outcome. Mental illnesses had disrupted our everyday lives and inserted us in this temporary holding cell, with the future yet unknown. I don't mean to discount the differences between being on the streets with a mental illness and my circumstances, but the commonalities mean more than the differences. All of us found ourselves overcome by our mental health conditions and couldn't cope on our own. We all ended up needing the additional support of a mental health facility to learn how to center ourselves.

My thought patterns proved I wasn't a normie. During my first visit to the psych ward, I came face-to-face with all my insecurities and inconsistencies in the way I viewed myself. Because I had nothing to do with large segments of my evenings after the daily activities ended, I had nowhere to hide from my thoughts. I realized that I uncritically accepted every thought that came into my brain as if I owned them, and this got me into big trouble. I had learned in my prior theological training and personal reading that the Holy Spirit, past traumas, and even demons can drop thoughts into our minds, and it's up to us to discern where the thought comes from. But in my own life, I ignored this practice. I believed that every thought about myself that came into my brain must be solid-gold truth and worth accepting. I'm guessing I shared this in common with my fellow patients—together, we found ourselves incapable of differentiating thoughts we should keep from thoughts we should discard.

Another thing we shared was perceived loneliness, even though we weren't truly alone. I observed that all of my fellow patients had visitors during my week in the mental health facility. Not a single person, not even those with no home to go to upon discharge, found themselves without advocates. These advocates included social workers, family members, pastors, and other community leaders; nobody was truly alone. Nevertheless, like everyone else in the psych ward, I felt completely abandoned and alone, left to my own devices by everyone who should care for me. This included my family, my friends, and my God. Part of me knew this to be false. After all, my friends kept me from attempting suicide and kept me safe until I could get to the mental health facility. Still, part of me still felt alienated from everyone and everything. And I'm confident that my fellow patients felt similarly, because we had some conversations about how lonely the psych ward feels.

My friend Joel (the one from the last chapter who helped me get admitted to the mental health hospital) told me a few months later that my admission to the psych ward caused him to reevaluate the way he viewed mental health conditions. Like my fellow patients, he had been operating under the assumption that "normal people" don't have problems with suicidality. He thought and expected that the people he worked with daily were somehow "other" than him and his friends. He reevaluated this based on our interactions, though. He respected and counted me as a close friend, and he thought I had plenty of stability in my life, but I had a mental health emergency. It caused him to realize that he misrepresented in his mind the people he served. He "othered" them to protect himself and create a sense of distance from his patients when in reality anyone could fall victim to a mental health crisis. Mental health never discriminates based on socioeconomics, race, creed, religion, sexuality, or anything else. It chooses whomever it wants.

What I Learned

Put simply, I learned I'm no normie. I'm just as messed up as every other patient in the psych ward with me. It took a while for me to come to grips with this reality for the simple reason that many of my fellow patients had a dual diagnosis, which means they had both a drug addiction and a mental health condition. I figured this out by watching them and by talking to them because almost everyone opens up about why they're in the psych ward. At first, I held myself at a distance from the dual-diagnosis individuals because (I'm ashamed to say this) I thought I was made of better stuff than them somehow. As I learned more about my fellow patients in our group sessions though, I learned that our struggles and our motivations had more similarities than I imagined. Many turned to drugs to cope with their mental health conditions, or conversely developed depression or anxiety as a function of their failed previous recovery attempts. I saw no shame in their stories, only the sadness of a life that took some wrong turns. I learned that jobs were lost, houses repossessed, marriages ended, and family relationships cut off because of these challenges. Instead of judgment, I felt compassion welling up in my heart. Depending on what happened to me in the next few years, there was no reason to say I might not end up just like one of my fellow patients, turning to drugs to soften the blow of my mental health condition. It made sense to me and surprised me all at the same time.

As I leaned into this common experience, I found support and strength from my fellow patients. I listened to how one man, who I'll call Eddie, never gave up, and I found myself inspired. He had been off drugs several times but always ended up back on them when times turned rough for him. He had been off drugs seven days when I met him and knew this would be the time that would stick. I asked myself, *Would I have such a positive attitude if I had failed so many times before?* The answer stood as an obvious *no* for me, and I found myself challenged to be more resilient in my life. But it wasn't just Eddie who taught me to be resilient. Everywhere I looked, I found people who had their lives ripped to shreds before their very eyes, yet they refused to give up. They continued to press forward toward a better future, even though their present and their past might be considered a disaster. This caused me to look at my own life and reevaluate it. My fellow patients inspired me to keep moving forward. If not for their testimonies of picking themselves up and trying again, I might have given up. Thank God for their examples.

Why It Matters

At the end of the day, none of us are normies. All of us are fallen creatures who are prone to sin and mistakes and shameful encounters in our lives. There's no distinction between the haves and the have-nots in the Christian life. We all fall under the same condemnation of sin and are all offered the same reconciliation to God through the sacrifice of Jesus upon the cross and his resurrection. It's so tempting to segregate the world into different categories and evaluate each category based on its own merits, but God doesn't operate this way. Humility should be the posture we take, whether we are currently struggling with a mental illness crisis or not. We never know what the future will hold for us or how we will emotionally respond to the new challenges that come our way.

Let me give you a quick example. One of my dear friends was in a completely stable place several months ago and had no reason whatsoever to believe that she would start struggling with her mental health. Then within the ensuing four months, two of her children received a chronic health diagnosis, another one of her kids started having marital problems and dumping on her, and another child tried to die by suicide. My friend entered into a crisis herself, and I woke up to a text asking, "When do I know when I need to admit myself to the mental health hospital?" I called her immediately to help her assess if she was a danger to herself and if she needed to go to the psych ward, but she wasn't at risk of a suicide attempt. Over the next several months, she and I have been in regular contact as her mental health has wavered based on her

> *While maintaining a stance of humility won't keep us from being thrust into an unexpected set of circumstances, it will ensure that we aren't battling questions of identity and worth through the process.*

ever-worsening circumstances. She continues doing her best just to stay above water, and some days that's pretty hard. I tell you this story to underscore this fact: we never know what's coming in our lives.

First Corinthians 10:12 says, "If you think you are standing strong, be careful not to fall." Put a different way, this verse tells us to stay humble, because life has a way of throwing curveballs we aren't expecting at us, and we never know how we are going to respond. While maintaining a stance of humility won't keep us from being thrust into an unexpected set of circumstances, it will ensure that we aren't battling questions of identity and worth through the process. My friend above did have some serious struggles, but her identity and worth as a child of God weren't among them. She kept that attitude of humility throughout her life, instead of thinking of herself as above struggles.

Another consideration can be found in Isaiah 35:3–4—"With this news, strengthen those who have tired hands, and encourage those who have weak knees. Say to those with fearful hearts, 'Be strong, and do not fear, for your God is coming. . . . He is coming to save you.'" We can enhance our humility by keeping an eye out for moments in which God might be coming to save those he loves. We discover these moments by looking for tired hands, weak knees, and fearful hearts. Our God restores those who are weary and fearful. We can see this throughout the pages of the Bible and in the lives of those we know. As we look for those who are struggling, we can enter into prayer for them, asking God to demonstrate his saving power in their lives. This will keep us humble because it will remind us that God is the one who saves. Not us.

How It Applies

1. Have you ever felt like a normie? How did that feel?
2. When you consider that none of us are really normies, what does that stir in your heart and mind?
3. How often do you struggle to remember and activate the idea that not every thought that enters your head actually belongs to you? What do you do to counteract that struggle?
4. Have you ever been in a season where it felt like thing after thing after thing kept going wrong, and how did you stay afloat during that time?
5. How often do you struggle to maintain an attitude of humility in comparison to others?

What God Thinks

With this news, strengthen those who have tired hands, and encourage those who have weak knees. Say to those with fearful hearts, "Be strong, and do not fear, for your God is coming. . . . He is coming to save you."

Isaiah 35:3–4

Maybe you're not the person who feels like they're in a place where they can humbly be praying for God to rescue the tired, weak, and fearful. Maybe instead you find your own hands tired, your own knees weak, and your own heart fearful. Let me start by saying this: it's okay to be here. Remember, there is no condemnation for those who are in Christ Jesus, and nobody else judges you either (or if they are judging you, they don't count because they're wrong).

Instead of slinking away in sadness or presuming that you aren't worth God's time, choose instead to step forward in whatever level of faith you have right now and ask God to save you. Make this simple prayer your own, because there's no magic in the particular words. Pray something like this:

God, I've read Isaiah 35, and I confess, that's me. I want to believe you're coming to rescue me, and part of me does believe that, but part of me also doesn't. Would you come and meet me in the gap between my belief and my doubt? Amen.

9

A(nother) Near-Death Experience

Yahweh! The LORD! The God of compassion and mercy! I am
slow to anger and filled with unfailing love and faithfulness.

Exodus 34:6

My Story

A week after I admitted myself, I stumbled out of the psych ward.
They said I should be ready to face the world again, and that my
suicidal thoughts seemed to be under control. I wasn't so sure. I
knew the demons that I still faced every morning, every night, and
every moment in between. But I was apparently ready to go back
out into the world. I found the first few days incredibly rough. The
psych ward had reduced my existence to watching bad television,
attending group therapy, and lying on my bed to sleep or read.
Now, I had a full house of kids who loved me, but I'd forgotten how
to engage with them. I had a wife who wanted to know I would

be okay, but I didn't know what to say to her—because I didn't feel okay. Amazing how much my life changed in a single week.

But I pushed forward, trying to put back together the pieces of a life shattered by suicidal thoughts. The day I admitted myself to the mental ward was different from any other moment in my life. Sure, I'd considered suicide before, but not like this. I knew I was going to die that day. I knew it, and so did everyone I talked to, everyone who played a part in me still being here today. I'm so grateful to the family and friends who surrounded me with phone calls and visits and, most importantly, love. They reminded me that I mattered and that the world would be a lesser place without me in it. Because that's the biggest lie that my suicidal thoughts told me. They said everyone would be better off if I wasn't around.

Coming back from the bland surroundings of the mental ward and reckoning with the wounds my suicidality had imprinted on my soul proved difficult. Some days, I found myself almost afraid to engage with anyone, in case I fell back into suicidal thoughts again. I didn't want to raise anyone's hopes about my future as a friend, or father, or husband, or . . . whatever, if I would just kill myself anyway. I found myself pulling away from my friends and family, almost as a courtesy to them for the next inevitable suicide attempt. Because I didn't trust myself to be able to say no the next time the opportunity presented itself. And I didn't want to deepen their pain by drawing closer to those I loved, only to rip myself away from them when I died by suicide later.

But I realized over time that every time I turtled up, I increased my chances of ending up back in the psych ward or dead. So, I slowly made the daily decision to live an open life. I uncovered the powerful truth that depression doesn't thrive in community. So, I chose to share the thoughts rumbling around in my head, even if they weren't good or safe or Christianly. I talked with my friends about the darkness as it descended on me, whether it overwhelmed me or visited me as a light touch. I invited God into the mix by praying when I felt off-center, and I began to develop daily routines that helped me find rhythm in each day. Together, these things staved off a battalion of depressive thoughts. And I also found something surprising to me—the people who loved me accepted these painful and distressing thoughts with gratitude. Don't get me wrong: they weren't happy I continued to battle suicidal thoughts, but they were thrilled I opened up to them. And they gave me plenty of ideas and tools in the fight for my life.

So I started using those weapons to fight the darkness. I began practicing centering prayers. I began to do body check-ins and to stop accepting as my own every thought that entered my brain. And an unexpected thing started to happen. I realized that I wanted to live again, and I stopped being afraid of the next time the darkness came knocking on my door.

And the darkness did come, with a fury I didn't expect. I spent the night at my mom's house. She has guns. It's a legitimate need because she lives on the far side of nowhere, where snakes and rabble-rousers abound. But I found myself in a bedroom at two o'clock in the morning, by myself, with a loaded gun on the night-stand. Before I knew it, I had the gun in my hand, pointed in my mouth. I was right back where I'd started, I thought. Here we go again, except this time there's no stopping me. I will die by suicide. There's nobody to stop me, nobody to call. It's just me, with a gun in my mouth. At that moment, two things came to my mind.

I remembered the people who matter in my life—my wife, my kids, my mom, and so many others who have become family even if they aren't blood relatives. They have been through so much with me already—and not just the battles. I thought of the moments of side-splitting laughter, the moments of unadulterated joy, and the moments of celebration. If I pulled the trigger, I would miss them all dearly. I wasn't ready to stop making memories with them.

And then, I thought about what would happen to my family if I chose to die by suicide. Stories from two of my friends came to mind. They'd told me how the wounds of suicides in their families have never healed, even decades later. One friend talked about his father committing suicide thirty years ago, and how he would never be okay, no matter how much time passed. I didn't want to hurt my loved ones so deeply and leave wounds that would never heal.

With these things in the forefront of my mind, I put the gun down. I started crying because part of me didn't want to put the gun down. But a bigger part of me knew that I wanted to live because I knew what I had to live for. This experience might sound like a failure to you. I saw a gun, and I shoved it in my mouth and contemplated dying by suicide. Again. But that's not how I see it. I see it as a victory. Here's the truth: I was by myself, with zero support and every opportunity to end my life. But I didn't. I fought back. On my own. Without anyone to tell me why. I battled with my own strength for my life. And I won.

What I Learned

There are two lessons I learned from this terrifying moment in my life, and they seem contradictory, but they truly aren't. I learned that suicidal ideations won't just disappear in my life, so I need to prepare accordingly. I also learned that the steps I'd been taking to build a stronger life could work. Let me explain.

A typical person isn't going to think *suicide* when they see a gun in the middle of the night on the nightstand, but that's all I could think about once I noticed it. I wasn't even trying to notice the gun at all. I had gotten up to use the restroom and happened to see it as I started to lie back down, and then I couldn't get the gun out of my mind. The thoughts came at me a million miles a minute, sounding a lot like this: *That gun would be the perfect way to end your life. It's even better than pills because you won't have to worry about the gun not working. You can guarantee the end of your life in an instant. It's the perfect solution to all your problems, Chris.* Before I even knew what happened, I had the gun in my hand and pointed it at my mouth. It seemed like it all took

100

place in a split second, as though no time had passed between the thought and the actions. I sat there stunned that this had taken place, but now I had to deal with the ramifications of this moment. Would I pull the trigger, or would I choose life?

Here's the second lesson I learned. I unwound the stories being told to me in my brain and recognized them as falsehoods. I could see that no "perfect way" to end a life early exists, because life shouldn't end early. I could look outside myself and see how this decision would destroy my family in so many ways for such a long time. And underneath it all, I could see that God still wrote my story, that somehow underneath all the pain, he wasn't done with me yet. So by sheer force of will, I put the gun down and went back to sleep.

I'd like to tell you I slept restfully, but that would be a lie. All night, temptations bombarded me to pick that gun back up and to "finish what I started." In a weird turn of events, these intrusive thoughts even insinuated that I wasn't a real man because I couldn't find the nerve to pull the trigger. But I persevered through the worst night of my life and made it to morning. Then I told my mom what had happened and asked her to remove the gun from the room, which of course she did immediately. I had to explain to her that it wasn't her fault she left the gun on the nightstand, and I wasn't holding her responsible for my suicidal moment. It's not normal to think about killing yourself when you see a gun unless you have some suicidal history, and I didn't expect or even want her to know how to think like me.

Why It Matters

Did you know that Moses once asked God to kill him? He got so fed up with the complaints of the people of Israel that he demanded that God take his life to spare him from misery. You can find this sobering, unexpected event in Moses's life in Numbers 11. After God started sending manna down from heaven every day for the people to collect and eat, they began to complain about having the same food every day. They longed for the variety of vegetables and meat from Egypt and voiced their complaints to God. We pick up the story in Numbers 11:10–15:

> Moses heard all the families standing in the doorways of their tents whining, and the LORD became extremely angry. Moses was also very aggravated. And Moses said to the LORD, "Why are you treating me, your servant, so harshly? Have mercy on me! What did I do to deserve the burden of all these people? Did I give birth to them? Did I bring them into the world? Why did you tell me to carry them in my arms like a mother carries a nursing baby? How can I carry them to the land you swore to give their ancestors? Where am I supposed to get meat for all these people? They keep whining to me, saying, 'Give us meat to eat!' I can't carry all these people by myself! The load is far too heavy! If this is how you intend to treat me, just go ahead and kill me. Do me a favor and spare me this misery!"

In other words, Moses allowed a frustrating moment to get the best of him and overreacted, but he overreacted directly to God. This wasn't an empty cry, because Moses complained to someone who could answer his request. God could have taken his life in that moment to answer his prayer. But God looked behind the request to die and saw the dual reasons for Moses's frustration. Moses was aggravated that Israel whined about not having meat. But there was a deeper issue at work here too. Moses found himself overworked because he managed all the needs of millions of people—simply too much for a single person to handle. In his wisdom, God addressed both issues. He gave Moses seventy people to share the burden of leadership with, and he also gave Israel meat. In other words, God responded gently and wisely to Moses's distress and met both the primary and the secondary needs.

God does the same with us in our trials and distresses. When I had that gun in my mouth, God might not have spoken directly to me in an audible voice, but he did bring to my remembrance the reasons I had to live. He dealt gently with me and met my unspoken need to stay alive. Even though I sat there ready to die, God pushed me to live by bringing my friends and family to mind. I know God will meet your needs just like he met my needs and Moses's needs because our God never changes. We can trust him to be faithful even when it seems like things are falling apart because he says he is trustworthy and has proven himself to be so.

How It Applies

1. Have you ever been in a season when you felt as though getting back into the normal routine of life seemed overwhelming and inconvenient? How did you recover from it?

2. What are your best tools right now for staving off depressive thoughts when they come at you?

3. Have you ever felt like depression or suicidality moved faster than your thoughts and you ended up in a precarious position as a result? What did you do next?

4. How difficult do you find it to believe that God can handle our frustrations? Do you feel like you need to keep everything sanitary with God?

5. Do you believe God deals gently with you? Why or why not?

What God Thinks

The LORD is merciful and compassionate, slow to get angry and filled with unfailing love.

Psalm 145:8

The unfailing love of God is a constant in our lives, whether we're aware of him or not. Nothing separates us from his love in Christ.

103

There exists no action we can take, no prayer we can pray, and no thought we can think that will shock God or cause him to give up on us.

This profound love can be a source of strength for us in our weakest moments and can support us when we feel all alone. There exists no action we can take, no prayer we can pray, and no thought we can think that will shock God or cause him to give up on us.

Believe me on this one—I've been to some crazy dark places, but God has gone to every place right along with me. I haven't always recognized him, but he's always been there, shining his hope and his light into my darkness. We have the privilege of being loved unconditionally by the Creator of the universe. Beyond his love, he demonstrates his gentle care with us as he did with Moses and with me. He will never "lose it" on us because of something we say or do but will always react out of kindness. He declares his love over us, again and again and again.

10

My Suicide Attempt

Everything that does not come from faith is sin.

Romans 14:23 NIV

My Story

Nothing had really changed in my life since the episode with the gun. I still found myself highly depressed, I slept a lot because of my depression, I wasn't actively doing anything to combat it, and I acted as though I was fine. I had moments when my healthy practices helped me overcome my depression, but if I'm honest, more days were down than up. Then things came to a head. The day after my youngest son's birthday, we were having a good time laughing about something downstairs. I had an intrusive thought at that moment that said, *Your pills are waiting for you upstairs. Now might as well be as good a time as any to take your life.* Shocked by the suddenness of this thought, I just accepted it as truth. As I look back, I'm embarrassed and sad to say that I didn't question this statement in any way. Even though we had a good time as a family, even though no emergency stressed me out, and even though everything was wonderful at the moment, I just accepted the thought as gospel truth.

I excused myself from the family and headed upstairs. I typed and printed two letters to my wife. One letter contained a series of instructions to help her put the pieces back together practically, covering things like website passwords and how to use my phone to pay bills. The second letter had an apology. I told her how much I loved her and how much I wanted to continue to build a life with her, but that I felt overwhelmed with sadness and grief about so many things and couldn't see a way through the pain. I tried to tell her it wasn't her fault, that I didn't blame her, and I wasn't unhappy with the life we had built together. I just needed the pain to stop, and I didn't see any other way. Then I downed about fifty pills, a combination of psychiatric medications and anti-seizure meds. I thought I knew from the research I had done earlier that this would be enough to kill me, and I needed to die in this moment.

The remainder of this chapter comes from a *very difficult* conversation I had with my wife about that day. I obviously don't remember what happened after I attempted, and frankly for much of the week after being admitted to the psych ward.

Some time later, my wife came upstairs to check in on me. She had assumed I had gone to bed because sometimes it was normal for me to go to sleep in the middle of the day without warning for no reason. She walked into the bedroom and saw the open pill bottles first. Then she saw me strewn across the floor, clearly having overdosed. Barbara told me that initially she found herself fueled by anger. I had promised her after my last psych ward visit that I would never attempt again, and here, two years later, I went through with the suicide attempt in the same way I had threatened to do it previously. She considered leaving me on the floor and letting the cards fall where they may, but eventually love won out over anger.

Her next dilemma: how to get me to the hospital. She wanted to avoid telling the kids that I had tried to die by suicide, so she tried to get me into the car on her own. As a frame of reference, I am 6'7" and nearly three hundred pounds, and my wife stands tall at 5'2". Quite the monstrous challenge. She managed to get me down the stairs with a little help from me, but my body gave out at the bottom of the stairs, and I collapsed. She had no choice but to call 9-1-1 at that point because she couldn't deadlift me to the car. The paramedics came and took me to the hospital, but because of COVID, nobody could go with me. As a matter of fact, they couldn't visit me at all in the psych ward for the same reason.

After the paramedics left, the real trial started for Barbara. She had to field questions from our kids and others about what I had done, why I had done it, and what would happen. She didn't really have any answers to any of those questions, which overwhelmed her. Barbara had to keep her nurse hat on throughout everything, so she couldn't process her own grief and anger because she needed to help everyone else process theirs. Then the waiting game began, when she had to keep on living life as if a major tragedy hadn't struck the family, and where she had zero information from anyone about me. She said that week was terrible for a million reasons, and I still regret causing that in her life. Eventually, I stabilized, and the doctors developed a plan of action to further stabilize me. Because my depression had proven to be treatment-resistant, which means I had tried multiple antidepressants to no effect, more dramatic action needed to be taken. The doctors recommended electroconvulsive therapy (ECT).

Let me pause for a moment to talk about ECT because there are a lot of misunderstandings about this treatment plan. In ECT, physicians use small amounts of electricity to direct the brain to reset the depressive episodes and give patients a chance to lead more successful lives. Television has done a real disservice to the medical community by making it appear that ECT is conducted on patients while they are awake, and that it involves a lot of pain and screaming. Although it is true that ECT patients in the past had significant changes in their behavior and personalities after the treatment, none of this held true for me. I was sedated and have little to no memory of the procedure at all, and I felt no pain from it at any point. My personality and behaviors have not changed, except that I am not as chronically depressed as I was prior to the treatment. So for me, ECT was a successful treatment option, along with the many other things we have talked about and will talk about in this book.

My wife joined by telephone as we discussed the next steps in my treatment. From what I understand, this conversation served as some of the first interactions with the physicians since my admission, so Barbara spent a good part of the week in the dark, wondering if I was even alive.

Then the worries about the specific treatment plan began. ECT has a history of success for treatment-resistant depression, but it's not without its own risks. I could lose significant portions of my working memory or worse, but we had honestly tried everything else already, so we had little choice. Barbara worried that I wouldn't be the same man she married because of these procedures and wondered if we would regret saying yes to them. In the end, I lost some of my working memory but remain largely the same man. Still, that didn't lessen the worry my wife had during this season.

What I Learned

Confession time: this is by far the most difficult chapter for me to write, for a few reasons. I've never committed a bigger sin, and it wrecks me every time I think about who I hurt, how much I hurt them, and how close I came to ending my life. It stirs up so many emotions for me when I think about this moment and those that followed. It's also difficult because I had to rely on my wife's memories for part of this chapter, which means we had to walk through her recollections. It reduced Barbara to tears and brought up some emotions that I wish I could have left alone. But I can't write a book on suicidal ideations without including this moment when I attempted suicide, so here Barbara and I walked through the pain together.

The first thing I learned: I can't be trusted around pills any more than I can be trusted around guns. I wasn't even in the room where the medication was, and their siren song of escape captured me and lured me into a suicide attempt. I'm obviously not blaming the pills—I made the choice—but we had to make some changes as a family after two suicidal moments with pills. Now everything except some allergy meds sits in a locked medication box, and I don't know where the key is. In the same way that my mom removed the gun as a temptation for my suicide brain, my wife has removed the pills as a temptation for me. I'm not going to lie; it sometimes makes me feel like a child that I can't manage my own pills. Barbara unlocks the box and refills the pills for our family every weekend. I can observe, but I'm never left alone with pills. It's for my own protection and to safeguard the family from further bad decisions I might make if given the chance.

It gutted me to learn that my wife thought about just leaving me on the floor because of her anger. Don't get me wrong, I earned that response. Still, it hurt that a decision I made caused so much pain for Barbara. I made a different kind of decision when I learned about this the first time. I drew a line in the sand and swore to myself and to God that I would never attempt suicide again, no matter how dark things got. I didn't yet know how I would keep that promise, but I didn't want to hurt my wife like that again. I love her too much to cause such pain, and as I said above, I hate that I did it even once.

Why It Matters

As I reflect on this dark time, I can now discern the difference between the voice of God in my life and other voices. God always leads us to freedom. The Gospel of John says that the way of Christ is life and life abundantly, so I use that as a key to unlock the mystery of who might be talking to me at a given moment. If the thought I have leads to abundant life, then it's from God. If the thought leads me *anywhere else*, then it's not from God. This seemingly simple recognition took me years to understand. I was taught as a young child that logical thoughts are superior to emotions, so I thought the brain was an insurmountable weapon against life. I know now that's just not true, that our brains are just as susceptible to being taken advantage of as our emotions or our will.

So, think on this, dear reader, as you consider the thoughts that rumble around in your head. If the thought would lead you to abundant life, then you can be certain that God brought it up and it's worth dwelling on. If that thought doesn't lead you to abundant life, then look at it with suspicion. Now obviously not every thought has abundant life as its source—pizza isn't about abundant life but can still be on our minds, right? But if a thought seems to lead you to a dark place, a place of despair, or toward a decision that would hurt you and others, then you can call it out and ask a few more questions of the thought.

I want to be careful not to paint with too broad a paintbrush, though. There are hard thoughts and difficult conversations we need to have with God, ourselves, and others. Don't avoid those conversations because they don't seem to lead to abundant life. Many difficult conversations do indeed lead to a more abundant life because they bring unspoken things into the light, release problems to God, allow forgiveness, and restore broken relationships.

> *If the thought would lead you to abundant life, then you can be certain that God brought it up and it's worth dwelling on. If that thought doesn't lead you to abundant life, then look at it with suspicion.*

Proverbs 14:15 relates to this idea of looking for abundant life in the thoughts that enter our minds: "Only simpletons believe everything they're told! The prudent carefully consider their steps." While nobody wants to be called a simpleton, sometimes that's exactly what we are, especially if we are believing everything that crosses our minds. The goal should be prudence, and to consider our steps wisely. Only after considering it should we move forward with a decision.

What are we to do, you might ask, with the incredibly difficult seasons that everyone endures? This doesn't seem like abundant life at all, and it's in these seasons that the allure of suicide might be strongest. There are no easy answers because the world we live in is busted. Romans 8 tells us that the earth itself groans for its redemption, and I think we find connection with that groaning. We long for redemption from a broken life and are anxious for God to get on with completing what he started. The best thing I can offer comes from Romans 8:18—"Yet what we suffer now is nothing compared to the glory he will reveal to us later." Like you, I don't know exactly what that glory God will reveal will look like, but I can tell you that it stirs hope in my heart. I remind myself that Paul knew a thing or two about suffering, and yet he knew that God's revealed glory remained greater than all his suffering. If he can hope in this, so can I and so can you.

How It Applies

1. How close have you come to a suicide attempt? What brought you there?

2. Do you connect with my wife's anger upon finding me upstairs after overdosing, and what are your thoughts about her response?

3. If you have ever had suicidal ideations, how difficult did you find it to separate your thoughts and consider which

might be leading to abundant life and which might not be leading you there?

4. How easy is it for you to be prudent in your steps?

5. How challenging do you find it to wait in your suffering for the glory God promises to reveal? What's specifically the hardest part for you in that?

What God Thinks

There is a way *that seems* right to a man, but its end *is* the way of death.

Proverbs 14:12 NKJV

This verse speaks directly to suicidality. Sometimes the only way forward seems to be a suicide attempt because life feels so bleak and the pain feels like it won't ever go away. This way seems to be the right way in our minds, but it ends everything God wants for us by bringing death. Instead of abundant life, it brings nothing but death. If you find yourself suicidal today or recently, I invite you to ask God to show you where his abundant life could be present in your life. I also plead with you to not choose suicide and to tell someone what you're feeling. It's hard to find God when darkness surrounds us, but he never leaves us without a witness in our lives. Allow this prayer to guide you in seeking the goodness of God today, right now:

God, I don't see abundant life anywhere I look. Suicide makes sense right now, if I'm being honest, but a part of me doesn't want to go there. Give me your eyes for my life, so I can see what you see in me and in my life. I need to see evidence of this abundant life you promise because I only see darkness.

God answers these prayers, if we only wait on him with whatever level of faith we have. He longs to engage us in these

112

life-and-death situations, and he won't disappoint us. Don't leave this in only God's hands, though. Reach out to a friend and tell them what you're feeling. If you don't feel like you have any safe friends, then call 9-8-8 and talk to a trained support counselor there. Trust me, you'll eventually be glad you didn't give in to these thoughts.

11

In the Psych Ward Again

So now there is no condemnation for those who belong to
Christ Jesus.

Romans 8:1

My Story

Ice-cold shame crushed my chest with its suffocating weight as I
regained consciousness in the hospital psych ward.

I slowly replayed the suicide attempt in my head. I'd tried to
overdose using a few medications that I mistakenly thought would
end my life.

I tried to die by suicide within a couple days of my son's birth-
day, I realized with a dull wince. *He'll have that memory forever*
superimposed on his birthday.

I felt like an utter failure. And the worst part? I found myself
angry I was still alive.

My pain, confusion, unresolved grief, and anger still waited
for me. Nothing had changed. *I can't even die by suicide right,*

115

I thought, adding that to the list of things I had angry thoughts about.

I felt so lost in the psych ward, in such a daze that I couldn't function. I went through the motions of taking whatever medications they placed in my hands, eating the food put in front of me, and zoning out in front of the television outside of required activities.

But after a few days, in an instant, everything changed.

I sat in the TV room half paying attention to a movie when I felt a stirring in my spirit. I didn't quite know how to process the feeling, but I knew I couldn't do anything while watching a movie, so I shuffled back to my room and sat on the bed. There in the middle of the psych ward, in the middle of my perfunctory existence, in the middle of my not caring about much of anything—God spoke to me. It felt simple yet profound, and it changed the trajectory of my life. I didn't hear an audible voice, but it might as well have been out loud.

God spoke into my heart, "I still love you."

I couldn't believe it.

Actually, I didn't believe it at first. I argued with him about this stunning revelation. "You can't love me—I tried to die by suicide. I'm a mess. I don't really even care if I'm alive right now. I don't want to talk to my wife or kids. I'm content to stay in this hospital for the rest of my days, except that means I can't attempt again. You can't love me. *I* don't even love me."

And I heard it again: "I still love you."

God didn't engage with any of my arguments. He didn't try to outwit me or talk me into a corner. He didn't do anything but declare his love for me, despite my current situation.

I wish I could tell you this whisper became all I needed to get on the road to recovery, but that's not the truth. My pastor came to visit me the next day. When I heard he'd come, I found myself incredibly nervous about what he would say to me. I recalled the previous conversations I'd had with other pastors about mental

> *Your family needs you. Your church needs you. We need you.*
> *The church isn't the full church without you in it. And God's not*
> *done with you yet.*

health, and how poorly they'd gone. Surely this would be more of the same—only worse because I'd actually attempted suicide.

I rehearsed these thoughts and prepared for the worst while walking down the hallways to the visitor room. I felt sick to my stomach, and I'd convinced myself that my pastor only came to heap condemnation on me. As a matter of fact, I almost turned around and headed back to my ward before I even reached the room. I only kept going because my current pastor seemed to be the type of guy who *might* not kick a brother when he's down. But if I'm being honest, I wasn't sure if I judged him rightly.

When I got to the room, Pastor Marty gave me a fierce bear hug. Then he said, "I'm sorry things got so rough for you that you felt you had nowhere left to turn but to try to end it. I've been closer to that place myself than I'd like to admit, and I know how it feels."

I wasn't expecting that. We talked some about the psych ward, if I liked the food (I didn't), and if I liked the people (they were okay).

Then Marty got down to business. I could see his demeanor change, and I prepared myself to be bulldozed again by a Christian leader. Only the bulldozing never came.

Instead, he looked me straight in the eyes and said, "We can't have this happen again. Your family needs you. Your church needs you. We need you. The church isn't the full church without you in it. And God's not done with you yet."

I could have taken this as an attack, but I knew exactly how Marty meant it. He wanted me to remember that the church was my family. This changed my life forever. God's whisper in the psych ward told me he still loved me—Marty's words affirmed me in a different way.

My pastor called me back to belonging, to a place called home. He reminded me my world is bigger than I'd felt it to be when I attempted suicide. Beyond that, he brought the reinforcements of hope and family to my soul and called me into a stronger sense of self-worth. I'm forever grateful to Marty for those words because they put a boundary line in my spirit that will keep me from attempting suicide again.

These became the kernels of hope I needed to rebuild my life. If God could still love me after my attempt, and if my pastor saw a reason to continue to invest in me, maybe I could be redeemable after all. Maybe my family could still learn to forgive me and love me again. Maybe I had a reason to try again. And that's what I did. Instead of being a zombie in our group sessions, I actively engaged, responding and asking questions. When the doctors came and interviewed me, I sat as an open book rather than a locked-up warehouse. When they suggested a very specific treatment, I questioned them about its efficacy, risks, and potential outcomes. I wanted to get better, and I remained willing to do whatever it took to get there. We did end up following that treatment, and it became exactly what I needed to break the ever-deepening cycle of depression that had been enveloping my life. But I wouldn't have even cared enough to learn about it without that whisper in my spirit and the visit from my pastor.

What I Learned

In only two days, my life rearranged—and it's lasted. The Holy Spirit spoke life into my bones with a simple declaration. It's something I could have read in any Bible, but it reverberated into the very depths of my spirit because I didn't read it, I felt it. Then my pastor affirmed the importance of my presence in my church and reminded me that I had a place to belong. My suicide attempt hadn't rendered me useless or unworthy of community. No, I was still wanted and needed in the place I called home. In the

118

sometimes-rocky roads that I've traveled since my hospital stay, these moments have been an anchor to my soul.

These realities have stayed my heart many times since then. I've had moments when I've wondered again if suicide might be the best option because I just can't seem to keep my head above water emotionally. I've considered whether tuning out of life for a few days and dwelling in the darkness of depression could be a viable path forward. Every time, I'm called back to these profound moments. I remember God still loves me and that he's not done with me yet. I reconcile my thoughts with the reality that my church needs me and isn't complete without me. And the recollections of these revelations from the tender heart of God almost physically force me to reenter my world.

With these reminders in my proverbial back pocket, I find the strength to move forward instead of giving up. The ever-present love of God calls me back to my day and doesn't allow me to settle into a routine of darkness or dissociation. Even though I haven't had God repeat himself to me again as he did in the psych ward that day, my spirit has been marked by the surrealness of that moment. God may as well be speaking afresh to my heart that he still loves me. It's new to me every time I consider it, and God refreshes me every time by his kindness toward me. More than his kindness, his steadfast love for me strikes me. God hasn't given up on me, even when I want to give up on myself. No, he has committed himself to me wholeheartedly and doesn't plan to walk away any time soon.

The support and encouragement of my pastor are just as profound for me in the moments when I'm tempted to turn back toward depression and suicidality. As you know because you've read my story, I've had my share of pastors who have given up on me or told me to be a better Christian to overcome my problems. They've told me to grow up and that my challenges would go away. Instead of that, Pastor Marty invited me back into the community of our church, regardless of my circumstances. He reminded me

119

that the way community works is that we come with our strengths *and* our weaknesses, and we give all that we have to each other in interdependence. Then the Holy Spirit shows up and bridges the gaps we can't manage on our own. He reminded me I need that, and I am needed in that, because the church only functions healthily when everyone participates together.

I'm no longer willing to coast through life in a fog, unengaged with my family or my friends. I don't want to miss the moments that make life worth having because I've been so close to losing them. I want to figure out how to invest more deeply in my local church community, to find my niche and my space to belong within it, because I believe what Marty told me—I believe the church needs me to be at full strength. So when I feel myself fading into the background or settling for a less-than existence, I internally straighten up and get back out into the world. You see, I've been accused in the past of not engaging even when I'm not suicidal, and I'm trying not to be that person anymore. It's time to be a fully engaged human in this life God has given me.

Why It Matters

Life should be seen as a gift from God. We can trace this idea all the way back to the garden of Eden. God told Adam and Eve to be fruitful and multiply. He didn't tell them to be sorrowful. He didn't tell them to regret living. He didn't tell them to mope. No, he gave them a purpose and told them to get about performing that purpose. It's the same with us. We have a purpose, and we are to go about doing it.

But our emotions or our depression or other mental health challenges can cloud our view of this purpose, and often we think that God will be angry or disappointed in us when this happens. If you're feeling that way, I have great news for you. There's an example in Scripture of exactly this thing happening, and we can see how God deals with people who are at their wit's end, ready to call it quits on life and throw in the towel. It's time to take a closer look at the prophet Elijah. He could have been bipolar, or at the very least had a major depressive moment.

Elijah had just participated in a tremendous victory with God against the prophets of Baal. In a prophetic showdown, both Elijah and the prophets of Baal had called upon their God to burn a sacrifice with fire from the heavens. In case you're not familiar with the story, Elijah won because God showed up with fire and Baal didn't.

But this victory had a high cost—the king and queen worshiped Baal, so Elijah had to flee for his life. He came to a tree in the middle of the desert and sat down. Then in 1 Kings 19:4, he cried out to God, "I have had enough, Lord. . . . Take my life, for I am no better than my ancestors who have already died." Just like Moses, Elijah became so upset that he asked God to kill him. I've been there, so I understand his sentiment. Let's see how the Lord answered his prayer (hint: God didn't kill Elijah).

Elijah fell asleep under the tree and woke up to an angel preparing a meal for him. He ate and drank this heavenly hash, then traveled for forty days to Mount Sinai, the mountain of God. Here's where things got really interesting.

God asked Elijah, "What are you doing here?" (1 Kings 19:9).

Elijah spoke out of his despair, stating that he'd zealously served the Lord but found himself all alone and in danger.

Then God asked him again, "What are you doing here?" (1 Kings 19:13).

Elijah again spoke of his despair, loneliness, and fear.

After this, God gave Elijah specific tasks to do—anoint some kings and anoint his successor to the office of prophet. Elijah left the mountain cave and got back to work.

So, how does all of this apply to you and me, you might ask? When God sees that we are at the end of our rope and despairing of life, he never agrees with our pleas for death. Instead, he guides us to rest and physical recovery as he did with Elijah. Then he invites us to engage with him out of a place of intimacy. In intimacy, we can make our laments known to him. He won't judge us or get angry at our pleas. Instead, he will listen, and then he will give us a job, like he did with Elijah. And he will give us the strength and courage to move forward into that destiny.

How It Applies

1. Have you ever been overcome with shame about where your mental health is? If you have, write down a few paragraphs about this or share it with a friend. If you're going through this book with a group, share this moment with the group.
2. Have you ever been angry that you're still alive, like Elijah and like the author? What brought you to that place of frustration?
3. Describe what home looks and feels like to you. What are the sights, smells, and sounds of the place that makes you feel safest in the world?
4. What does it mean to you to believe that God has a job for you to go about doing? What might that job specifically be for you?
5. When you read about how God treated Elijah when he felt deeply depressed and suicidal, what emotions do you experience?

What God Thinks

But the LORD said to him [Elijah], "What are you doing here, Elijah?"

1 Kings 19:9

God may very well be saying the same thing to you today: "What are you doing here?" Why are you where you are right now, instead of participating in the community known as the church and giving your strengths and weaknesses to the work of God in the world? Nothing has disqualified you from doing your part, and you are needed for the church to be the church in all its strength.

You might be in a proverbial cave in the middle of a mountain, hoping to meet with God or just hiding from the world like Elijah. God might be calling you out of hiding and back into the work of showing his goodness in the world. Just like with Elijah, he might be inviting you to lament so as to draw near to him and hear afresh his calling on your life. Remember that God isn't afraid of your laments, and many times he waits for your laments to offer his hope and his restoration to you. He longs to have you share the things in your heart, because that's intimacy, and God longs for intimacy with each of us.

If you have a sense that this could be God's heart for you, I'd invite you to enter into that with gusto. Don't hold back anything from God, but instead lay your complaints at his feet. As he did with Elijah, God will hear those complaints, not be offended or frightened by them, and will give you a fresh anointing for the good works he has prepared for you. This becomes an opportunity to enter into intimacy with God—don't miss it out of fear or hesitation.

12

Restoring Family Relationships Takes Time

Your life is now hidden with Christ in God.

Colossians 3:3 NIV

My Story

I shuffled out of the psychiatric ward with my belongings in a clear plastic bag, walking with my wife to the car. So many questions remained unasked and unanswered between us, but the biggest one stuck out. *Why did you attempt suicide?*

There are so many things that I regret doing in the aftermath of my suicide attempt. I don't love how I responded to my family, and if I could do it over again, I'd do many things differently.

My wife took my attempt as a personal rejection of our life together. For me to attempt suicide, I must have been so disillusioned, so dissatisfied, and so angry with our life that it felt better to end it than to keep trying to improve it. It didn't make sense to her that I would choke down a pile of pills the day after our son's birthday unless things seemed hopeless in every way. Beyond that, she found herself full of fear that any questions might throw me right back into the hospital or, worse, trigger yet another suicide attempt. She was trapped between confusion and fear.

For my part, I didn't have the words to explain my feelings, so silence stifled the air in the car on our way home. I knew my wife had questions she wanted to ask me, but I found myself too tired to pull them out of her. Not that I blamed her for not asking them—it's not her fault that I tried to die by suicide.

When I got home, one of my sons acknowledged me with a fierce hug. He was glad I didn't die and told me as much. He could somehow hold in tension the idea that I was back and I love him, despite the suicide attempt. He seemed almost unfazed by things, in a way that still doesn't seem right. I almost felt like he might be missing something in my story somehow, even though he saw me unconscious on the floor after the overdose. Surely he had questions that he wanted to ask. He swore he didn't, so I let it go. I wish I hadn't. Because I didn't pursue this line of conversation with him, we unintentionally erected a barrier between us that took some time to tear down again.

My other son didn't give me a free pass, though. We had a forty-minute conversation where he peppered me with question after question: Why did you choose pills instead of a knife or a gun? Why this time of year? (I've struggled with the same time of year for a long time.) What exact thoughts went through your head when you decided to do it? Why did you do it with the family home so they would find you?

I did my best to answer his questions, but I knew he wasn't really satisfied. I could see the rejection and pain he felt, hear it beneath the questions. Broken by the conversation, I nevertheless felt like I deserved it after everything I'd put my family through.

I don't know which reaction hit me the hardest. The silence, the celebration, and the cynical quizzing all took their toll on me, mostly because I didn't have real answers for anyone.

Even though I'd basically done nothing in the psych ward but sit on chairs, attend therapy, and sleep, I felt so, so tired. I couldn't summon the strength to push through the silence, to ask about the hug, or to speak love to the hurt underneath the questions. I barely subsisted. Trying to process all these well-warranted feelings from my family all at once overwhelmed me. To be honest, I shut down after being released from the psych ward. It took me the better part of three weeks to find my rhythm again. I've talked with my family since then, but part of me wishes I'd been more prepared when I came home, that I could have answered the spoken and unspoken questions better. I've affirmed to my wife that I *love* the life we've built together and I'm proud of it. I've checked with my bear-hugging son to see if there are unspoken concerns about me, and I've talked with my questioning son about the same. We as a family have a much more open level of communication about my struggles now, and it's because I've recognized since my suicide attempt that they deserve this much from me, no matter how intense and difficult it might be for me.

If I'd known myself as well as I do now and if I'd understood how deeply my suicide attempt would hurt my family, I'd have handled things differently.

I'd been struggling with deep depression for the better part of three months when I attempted suicide, but I wasn't aware of how deeply it impacted me. Because I wasn't paying attention to myself, the onslaught of suicidal thoughts seemed to come from nowhere. I had zero context for what would happen next. I also had zero defenses prepared because I hadn't spent the time necessary to develop them. I thought I could float through life with a major mood disorder without having plans for what to do when things went awry. I know better now.

If I had a do-over of the day I came home, I would tell my wife right away it wasn't her fault. She didn't cause my suicide attempt by what she did or didn't do or say. To this day, she worries about bringing up sensitive topics. Whether it's a fight we're having, a

127

difficult conversation about something I'm doing professionally, or a quick decision about mealtime, she will sometimes feel like she's walking on eggshells. We've talked through the fact that I'm much more stable now, but she still worries and she doesn't know what might push me over the edge again. This has lessened over time, but she's told me it still crosses her mind, and this makes sense to me.

We've had some conversations since about why I ended up attempting suicide, but I took longer than I should have to start them. I was too exhausted from my recovery, trying to put the pieces of my life together, to invest immediately in our marriage. I wish I could take this back. We're still rebuilding trust because that's what my attempt felt like to her—a breach of trust. I wish I'd started the restoration process sooner because I love my wife with every fiber of my being. She's worth investing in, no matter how hard a conversation is.

My two boys processed my suicide attempt very differently—one with affection and the other with a cynicism bordering on anger. I understand both responses. I'd respond very differently to each of them if I had a do-over. I'm saddened that I stayed in answer-man mode with my questioning son. I never addressed any of his underlying hurt but instead focused very intently on giving him succinct, direct answers to his questions. If I'm honest with myself, I shut off my emotions and replied analytically, which wasn't what my son needed from me. He's in his head a lot of the time, and he needed to hear my heart. He needed to know I made a mistake: one I won't repeat. He needed to know that I love him despite my bad choice and that my choice wasn't about him. A difficult moment overcame me, and my decision in that moment will haunt me for the rest of my life. We've since had this conversation, and I have assured him that I'm situated in a stronger place emotionally and mentally than in 2020, so this shouldn't ever happen again. He's chosen to trust me again, which I'm grateful for.

With my other son, I'd give him space to just be with me and ask questions. Instead of focusing individually on my own shattered soul, I'd have invited him to join me in the repair of my life. This would have given him an opportunity to ask the questions I wonder if he still has in his own spirit. Together, we could have uncovered a fresh expression of friendship as we mourned the loss of things that used to be and built toward the future. Thankfully, we are bridging the gap in our relationship that I created by shutting him out initially, and I'm hopeful this gap will continue to lessen.

What I Learned

Suicide attempts always tear at the fabric of families because the pain and the fear of loss are deeply intense. My family is slowly healing, but it's *despite* the decisions I made when I came out of the psych ward, not because of them. In retrospect, I wish I'd been more intentional about involving my family in my recovery. We're slowly getting there, but we'd be that much closer to health and wholeness if I'd made different choices in the days following my release from the hospital.

I've learned since that my mental health disorder means I have a responsibility to talk with my family about my problems when they arise, or as soon after as I can. I abdicated that responsibility on the day I got out from the psych ward. I know this sounds overly harsh because I was exhausted, but it isn't. Because I love them so deeply, I owe it to my family to be "on" when they're ready to talk about my suicidality, whenever that comes up.

I particularly owed it to them on the back end of a suicide attempt. They weren't able to ask me their questions on the front end. Instead, they found me in the bedroom nearly unconscious, with two goodbye letters typed and printed. They watched as first responders came and took me to the hospital, and because of COVID, they couldn't go with me. They had to wonder if I would make it out alive. They deserved answers, but I didn't give them any.

I've learned from these mistakes, and I keep short accounts now with my family about my mental health. Instead of waiting until I feel like talking about it, I preemptively have conversations with them—with my wife in particular—whenever I feel a bit off. They deserve to know. I obviously temper the conversations depending on who I'm talking to. For example, my special needs daughter doesn't need to know all the ins and outs of my depressed brain. She can know that her dad feels extra sad and needs prayers, though—I've told her things like that before. But I recognize that I no longer have the right to withhold information about my mental health. My family thinks about it at least as often as I do.

Why It Matters

It's far too easy to look at events like suicide attempts with an eye toward shame and judgment. The Bible actually has a lot to say about how God views us when we make mistakes, and it might not give the answers you expected. Romans 8:1 says, "So now there is no condemnation for those who belong to Christ Jesus."

We'll come back to this core message, but let's set this glorious verse in context first. Romans 7 speaks about the struggle between making the right or wrong choice. Some scholars believe that this passage refers to a non-Christian's experience of life, but I disagree with them on both practical and theological grounds. The Christian life is full of moments like we find in Romans 7:15—"I don't really understand myself, for I want to do what is right, but I don't do it. Instead, I do what I hate."

Who hasn't been there, beset by sinful choices when we want to make the right decisions? Paul commiserates with all of us in Romans 7:24–25:

> Oh, what a miserable person I am! Who will free me from this life that is dominated by sin and death? Thank God! The answer is in Jesus Christ our Lord. So you see how it is: In my mind I really

130

want to obey God's law, but because of my sinful nature I am a slave to sin.

We desire to make the right choices and obey God, but we lack follow-through because of our sinful nature.

Let me pause right here and say something important: depression and suicidal ideation are not sinful. We're using this construct from Romans 7–8 to talk about challenging circumstances, not to call out depression or suicidal thoughts as sin. These moments are deeply personal and come from any number of life circumstances that have happened to us, and in almost every case we are responding out of our hurt or pain. We just want the hurting to stop. This comes as one particular result of a sinful fallen world, not out of our personal sinfulness.

It's equally important to call out the reality that making or executing a plan of suicide is sinful, yet even in this, God does not condemn us. Many in the past have said that suicide might be an unforgivable sin, but this is bound up in a poor theological understanding of how forgiveness works. It's based on a mostly Catholic perspective that we must formally repent of specific sins before we die to receive the forgiveness of Christ. A more biblical understanding says that the forgiveness Jesus offers covers all our sins—past, present, and future—regardless of when we specifically ask for forgiveness from them. Therefore, we are forgiven for our suicide plans, and they're not an unforgivable sin.

Okay, back to the text at hand. The immediate context of the promise in Romans 8:1 is Paul's struggle with decision-making in the heat of the moment. Paul writes about our often-defeated selves, and still he says there is no condemnation for Christians. Not only are we rescued from the despair of our failing attempts to live rightly, but we are freed from condemnation for the times when we don't make the best choices. This powerful statement has immediate application for us when we are suicidal or in the deep recesses of depression. When things aren't going well for

> *When God looks at us, he doesn't see our weaknesses, our mistakes, or our failings. He doesn't see our depression, our anxiety, or our suicidality. He sees Jesus. Only Jesus.*

us, it can feel like God gangs up on us alongside our own self-perceptions of how terrible we are as human beings. We might even picture God up in the heavens scolding us for not getting our lives together.

But that's not the story this verse paints. According to Paul, God does not condemn us. There's a beautiful theological image attached to this verse that's worth exploring. The righteousness and perfection of Jesus's life, ministry, death, burial, and resurrection are superimposed upon us when God views us so that all he sees when he looks at us is Jesus. Allow that to settle into your spirit. When God looks at us, he doesn't see our weaknesses, our mistakes, or our failings. He doesn't see our depression, our anxiety, or our suicidality.

He sees Jesus. Only Jesus.

What a powerful antidote to our feelings of inferiority in the middle of a depressive episode or when we're battling suicidal thoughts. God looks at us and views us with the same love that he has for his son Jesus. He never steps away from us or calls us unworthy. He always steps toward us in love and acceptance. This deep spiritual reality can give us the strength to step toward our family and friends in transparency to share our mental health struggles.

Knowing that God views us without condemnation can lend us the courage to have life-giving but profoundly difficult conversations with others. Understanding how God views us could be perhaps the single most important key to restoring family relationships. That might seem like an exaggeration, but it's certainly been true in my life. It's only as I've been able to dial in to this recognition of God's absolute acceptance of me that I've been able to risk having open conversations with my family.

How It Applies

1. When you have felt unable to process your own emotional state, what steps have you taken to get unstuck, and how successful have they been?

2. How transparent have you been with your family and friends about the depths of your struggles with your mental health condition? If you find that you haven't been very honest, what holds you back?

3. When you're recovering from a low season, how much energy are you able to invest in conversations with your family during your recovery, and do you have any regrets about how you've handled them?

4. What are your strategies when you feel as though God condemns you for your dark thoughts? Or, to put it differently, how do you respond when you feel attacked for struggling?

5. If you could let go of the inferiority that so often comes with depression and suicidality, what would change in your spiritual life?

What God Thinks

Thank God! The answer is in Jesus Christ our Lord.

Romans 7:25

All too often in Christian subcultures we're taught that Jesus is the answer to everything. We're expected to allow this simplistic statement to permeate our souls and solve our problems. Usually it's not enough to cover the darkness of this world. Pat answers aren't good enough for the things that happen in this world. Wars and unexpected deaths and COVID and chronic illnesses all cry out for a more nuanced response. I hate platitudes, and I'm convinced God does too.

But there's a powerful sense in which Jesus truly is the answer to the darkness in our own souls. If God only sees Jesus when he looks at us, perhaps we should try the same tactic. Instead of viewing ourselves through the lens of weakness or seeing ourselves as damaged goods, let's take a God's-eye perspective on things.

How differently would we think of ourselves if we saw only the righteousness of Jesus? What chances would we take in our lives if we believed we lived as the righteousness of God? How would our interactions with our loved ones change if we viewed ourselves as God does? Consider these questions for a few moments in silent meditation. It's a bit much to think that a few minutes of meditation are going to give you the power to suddenly start acting like the person God sees in you, because that's not how life works. But whenever shame creeps in or you know a hard conversation about your mental health might be coming up, you can meditate on this verse again and take courage in its powerful message.

13

My Great Counselor

Fools think their own way is right, but the wise listen to others.

Proverbs 12:15

My Story

I realized that life couldn't go on as it had been for the last decade. No more visits to the psych ward because I wasn't taking care of myself. No more suicide attempts that seemed like they were coming out of the blue to me. No more trying to make it on my own without the right kind of support. Things needed to change. I needed help—and a lot of it—if I would be able to rebuild my life on a firmer foundation than I'd been trying to for the last bit. I'll talk some in the next chapter about the specific steps I took after I found a *great* counselor for myself, but right now I want to focus on that counselor because he's literally been the difference between life and death.

In chapter 6, I talked about my bad experience with my first two counselors, so I had a lot of nervousness about returning to therapy again. Still, I knew that I needed the support. I couldn't trust myself to navigate the treacherous waters of my thoughts and emotions without professional help, so I started looking for a new counselor. I started by arming myself with the things I learned from my two false starts. This meant I couldn't have a person who wasn't equipped to deal with my seizures. Because of this, I decided that I wanted someone with a PhD level of training, as I assumed they would be more exposed to and familiar with the types of health problems I present when compared to someone with a master's degree in counseling. I needed somebody who would be at least open to my Christian faith, if not an actual Christian counselor, so I added that to my list. I decided as well that I wanted to try a male therapist, simply because my previous two were women. I have nothing against female counselors, but I thought it might make sense to try something different this time around. Armed with these categories of information, I revisited my insurance website. I put in these characteristics: PhD, male, and Christian. To my surprise, I saw only three options within twenty-five miles of my house. Maybe this wouldn't be as intimidating of a prospect as I thought!

I looked more closely at the three options that popped up for a counselor who met my qualifications. One only did telehealth appointments at the time. While this seemed perfectly reasonable because of the pandemic, it wouldn't work for me. I knew myself well enough to know that my attention would stray from the appointment if I didn't sit right in front of a therapist. ADHD at its best, working against me! So that left two therapists. The first one I looked at focused on helping men uncover their hidden masculinity and recover their God-given place in their families. I almost visibly recoiled, thinking of my previous church experiences and that pastor who told me that I was at fault for my depression. There was no way I could stomach a therapist with that approach to his counseling, so one option remained. I called and left a message for this counselor and anxiously waited a week for him to get back to me. Nothing. I almost gave up right then and there, because I had nobody left to reach out to. I knew I couldn't go on without help, so I called the counselor again. He picked up, and we scheduled an appointment for the next day.

I found my anxiety was through the roof about meeting him. All sorts of crazy expectations of disaster flew into my mind. First I assumed that he would gaslight me and tell me my depression wasn't real, and then I assumed that he would want to readmit me immediately to a mental health facility upon meeting me. Nothing like conflicting anxieties! Next I thought that he would be aggressive and angry with me, trying to assert his way into changing my behavior. None of this came true though when I finally met Glen. Instead, he presented as a mild-mannered, kindhearted, open-spirited former Catholic priest with a tender spot for people battling their demons. In other words, perfect for me.

In my first appointment, I laid out for him that I had been in a mental health facility twice in the last two years, once for suicidal ideations and once for a suicide attempt. I explained that I'd had several other moments where I'd battled suicidal thoughts too, and that I had been fighting this most of my adult life. I added to this the fact that I have seizures that could and likely would interrupt our sessions at some point, and that my faith mattered to me. To all of this, he simply said, "Chris, I believe I can help you. It won't be easy by any means, but I've helped many who are in situations like yours before. You're no longer alone. You can call or text my cell number at any time and I'll be here for you. I'm on your side, no matter what."

Relief flooded into my soul as I heard him say these words. He went on to talk about his background as a psychiatrist and psychologist, and he explained that he wouldn't be able to prescribe any medications to me because his licensure from Illinois doesn't allow him to do this in Arizona. But he committed again to being an advocate and support for me. He told me about his experience as a Catholic priest and a seminary professor, and how he moved on from the ministry to begin a career as a therapist. We began to build rapport almost immediately and I felt at peace with Glen. I knew I had found my counselor.

A few months later, this theory was tested. One of my friends, another mental health advocate, had been found dead in a hotel room after suicide. I wasn't okay because I had just talked to him the prior week and he seemed fine. It made me wonder how steady I might be and whether I should trust in my apparent stability. I texted Glen and told him what happened. As soon as he got home from running his errands, around 6:45 in the evening, we had a FaceTime call. He asked me for the details of the suicide, and I provided him with what I knew. He asked if I planned to go to the funeral, and I told him I didn't trust myself to go because I thought it would destabilize me. He asked if the family would notice my absence, and when I said no, then he agreed that I shouldn't go. Then he said, "You know what, Chris? Just because your friend fell after becoming a mental health advocate doesn't mean you will. Everybody walks their own path. Yours doesn't have to be his. Stand firm and you will be just fine." He addressed the fears I hadn't even shared with him yet because he understood how my heart and mind work, and I felt at peace. The next few weeks remained rough as the news spread about my friend's suicide, but I stood firm amid it all because I remembered the words Glen spoke over me. My path doesn't have to be the same as my friend's path. I have continued to see Glen over the last several years, and my trust in him has continued to grow. I know that in Glen I have an advocate and a shoulder I can lean on whenever it's necessary.

What I Learned

The biggest thing that I have learned from Glen over the last few years remains how to keep everything in perspective. The technical term is *cognitive reframing*, but Glen always tells me to keep things in perspective, so that's how I want to talk about it here. I tend to overthink and overreact to things pretty easily, and it gets me in trouble with my depression and suicidality. I didn't even realize this as a problem until I started meeting with Glen, but he's helped me to see how warped my thoughts often become because of my inability to cognitively reframe events or potential events.

Let me give you a simple example of something that recently happened in my life that shows you how out of whack things can get for me. I hadn't heard from one of my close friends for about three days, when we usually talk every day. I dropped her a quick note to see if we were okay. I heard nothing from her for another three days, and that's when I had my appointment with Glen. I convinced myself that Lindsay had become very upset with me and that she held off on talking to me because of this anger.

I expressed all this to Glen, and he responded by asking me a few questions. "Is Lindsay usually someone who would not talk to you about things when she's angry?"

"No."

"Is it possible that she's just been really busy—does that sometimes happen with Lindsay?"

"Yes."

"Is it more likely that she would talk to you about whatever bothered her, or that she would ignore you for a week?"

"She would talk to me."

Then he suggested that she was probably on vacation, overly busy, or sick. He told me I should pray for her in case it was the last one, but otherwise, just wait and see what happened since it was probably the first or second one. Two days later, Lindsay messaged me. She had been sick for the better part of a week and was just now recovering.

I wanted to declare our friendship dead when Lindsay was just sick. Without help from Glen, I would have been on high alert about my friendship with Lindsay the whole time, assuming the worst about things between us, when really what happened wasn't about me at all. I think that's the biggest thing I've learned about cognitive reframing. Not everything in this world revolves around me, not even the things in my life, much less the things in other people's lives. Life is far too complex for it to always be about me, and it's ridiculous for me to assume that. Instead, I bring logical questions to my spiraling emotions and ask if there are any alternatives. I tend to catastrophize, which is exactly what it sounds like—making something (or everything) a catastrophe, whether it deserves a catastrophic reaction or not. Armed with this new skill of cognitive reframing from Glen, I now take these moments of catastrophizing and walk back from the hypothetical cliff. It's much more likely that the end of the world isn't nigh, and I'm able to act like that now. It's still a very manual process, but it's a powerful tool in my toolbox when things get hairy in my life. I have specifically learned to ask the following questions:

1. Is this thing you are worried about necessarily true?
2. Is there a possibility that this situation isn't actually about you at all?
3. What other options are there that explain these circumstances?
4. How likely is each option, and can you figure out which one is true before you emotionally react to a potentiality?
5. If the worst-case scenario is actually true, what can you do about it right now?
6. If the worst-case scenario is not actually true, what benefit do you gain by worrying about this potential scenario?

These questions have empowered me to be able to look at a situation that feels out of control with reasonableness. I step back from the assumption that the world is ending and strategize about how to react to the situation instead. I gather more information or prepare for the most likely outcome. I bring my emotions back under control using rationality. Now, I want to be careful here. I'm not saying emotionality is somehow less than being rational because that's simply not true. In my experience, my emotionality gets the best of me when I can't slow down the catastrophizing enough to gauge how realistic the potential thing that I'm thinking about actually is. Your path might look different, but for me catastrophizing becomes best controlled by using cognitive reframing and stepping through the questions I listed above.

Why It Matters

The end goal here becomes learning to guard our hearts against catastrophizing. The Bible has a lot to say about guarding your heart. Proverbs 4:23 says, "Guard your heart above all else, for it determines the course of your life." How might guarding our hearts against catastrophizing be important? First, we need to guard our hearts because our hearts are valuable. Nobody guards their garbage pail, but too often we treat our hearts like trash. Our hearts are worth guarding because they are the wellspring of life. Jesus says springs of water flow from our hearts if we trust in him (see John 7:37–39). If our hearts are the source of our faith and our hope in Christ, plus so much more, then we certainly need to guard our hearts. This matters deeply.

Our hearts are the source of everything we do. In Matthew 15:18–19, Jesus says, "But the words you speak come from the heart—that's what defiles you. For from the heart come evil thoughts, murder, adultery, all sexual immorality, theft, lying, and

> *Nobody guards their garbage pail, but too often we treat our hearts like trash. Our hearts are worth guarding because they are the wellspring of life.*

slander." Not only do our words come from our hearts, says Jesus, but so do all sorts of sins. This makes sense if you think about it. Every sin begins with a thought, and biblically these evil thoughts originate in our hearts. So, it's vital for us to guard our hearts against evil to prevent sin from taking hold. In the context of catastrophizing, we can walk down a path of presumption and take actions we regret if we aren't careful. Imagine if I had, for example, sent an angry text to my friend Lindsay after five days of not hearing from her. Think how our friendship would have been impacted if I had blurted out something about her being angry with me or, even worse, if I had cut off our friendship because of some perceived offense. We must guard our hearts against catastrophizing to prevent sin from taking hold and walking us toward regrettable actions.

How It Applies

1. What are the key characteristics that you would need to have in a therapist?
2. If you have already done this, how did you find a counselor? If you haven't yet done this, what do you think your first step would be?
3. How much fear do you have about laying all your "dirty laundry" out in front of a relative stranger? What kinds of things would put you at ease when seeing a new or current counselor?
4. How often do you find yourself catastrophizing in your life?
5. What strategies have you found that work in battling the catastrophizing tendency?

What God Thinks

And now, dear brothers and sisters, one final thing. Fix your thoughts on what is true, and honorable, and right, and pure, and lovely, and admirable. Think about things that are excellent and worthy of praise.

Philippians 4:8

I can't say that I approached finding my great counselor Glen in light of this verse, but I found in him someone who has helped me to focus on precisely the things God has called me to think about. I would encourage you to do the same. A therapist holds a special place in our lives because of their training and expertise, but at the end of the day, there still needs to be spiritual fruit in that relationship for it to be useful and honoring to God. Perhaps even more than most other relationships, a counselor needs to hold our hand and walk us toward a godly way of approaching the events in our lives. If they can't help us see God, life, and hope in challenging times, then they aren't worth the time and energy (or money!) that we are investing in them. As you consider your current or future counselor, I'd encourage you to use Philippians 4:8 as a lens through which to evaluate them. Are they able to help you find true, honorable, right, pure, lovely, admirable, excellent, and praiseworthy things in your life, no matter how dark it seems to get? If they can do this, then you've found a great counselor just like Glen has been for me.

14

Rediscovering My Groove

Stand firm, and you will win life.
Luke 21:19 NIV

My Story

I received a text out of the blue from my pastor with zero context—he wanted to know how I was holding up. Surprised and confused, I told him I was doing fine and asked about the concern since I couldn't think of any reason for him to be worried. He told me that it was *that time of year* for me, and then I realized what he meant. You see, I've struggled with dark depression and suicidality in July and August for the better part of a decade. I have some thoughts on why that is, but it's all guesswork. Bottom line: that time of year has historically been very rough for me. But that's the good news in this story. Even though *that time of year* had come around again, I wasn't struggling at all, for the first time in I don't even know how long. I thanked my pastor for reaching out and let him know how successful I'd been lately in the battle against my depression. Then I started to wonder, *What has changed and why can I now be in a good place?* I realized at least three keys to the shift that had recently taken place in my life.

First, I established a morning routine that centered me at the very beginning of every day. These activities have helped me to start the day off on the right foot, even if I got out of bed on the wrong side. I start each morning by reading a short passage of Scripture and meditating upon it for a few moments. I don't spend an hour in the Bible—on the contrary, it's just enough to remind me that God is my center, he is my source, he is for me, he loves me desperately, and he is working for my good. From there, I engage in a short prayer where I dedicate my day to God and ask him to show me where he's moving and present in my life. I follow this brief prayer time with a podcast called *Pray Every Day* by Mary DeMuth. In this podcast, Mary reads a passage of Scripture and prays through it for herself and her listeners. From there, I take a moment to be mindful of what might be going on in my body, if I'm feeling any physical soreness or emotional agitation; then I lift these things up to God in prayer.

Finally, I practice some simple breath prayers.[7] As I close my eyes, I silently pray something with the intake of breath and something else on the exhale. Here are two examples: *Speak to me* on the inhale, followed by *Your child is listening* on the exhale; *Holy Spirit* on the inhale, followed by *Breathe on me* on the exhale. These short prayers center me on the activity of God happening in the moment and prepare me to stay focused on God throughout the day. Sometimes, I have a profound sense of God's presence as I breathe these prayers and it encourages me to stay centered on

7. If you're interested in learning more about breath prayers, and if you want a resource full of sample breath prayers for you to use, all in a beautiful package, I highly recommend Jennifer Tucker's book *Breath as Prayer: Calm Your Anxiety, Focus Your Mind, and Renew Your Soul.* I've been using it for a while now, and it's tremendous.

God. Other times, nothing happens. Either way, I'm learning to practice the presence of God in a practical way, and this bears fruit in my life.

Altogether, these morning activities take less than twenty minutes, but they allow me to start every day in a centered way. I do my best to start these practices as early as possible in my day, preferably before I've even eaten breakfast. The consistency of these practices has done wonders for me, primarily because mornings and I don't mix. I had a bad habit of letting a rough morning bleed into the afternoon and evening.

Second, I made a rock-solid commitment to a core group of friends to always be brutally honest with them about my emotional well-being. Instead of hiding my depression or suicidality from them in shame, I stopped shrinking back and instead stepped forward. I decided to take my friends at their word when they told me that they loved me, wanted me to stay alive, and wanted God's best for me. So I keep short accounts with my depression. As soon as I feel myself starting to slip, I begin talking with my core friends about it. Together, we diagnose what might be causing it, and I actively work to counteract the root of the problem. Sometimes it may be that I have stopped practicing my morning routine and I've had a few off-kilter days in a row that are making me unsteady; if that's the case, then it's simply a matter of reinstating those patterns in my life. There are other times when I'm allowing a relational scrum in my family to take up space in my spirit; then I have to either deal with the problem directly or choose to let it go, but I can't hold on to it indefinitely. Sometimes I don't know what's going on, but I just feel down. These are the hardest to diagnose because there's nothing that makes sense as an explanation. In these situations, I ask my friends to pray for me and keep close tabs on me, so I don't do something I'll regret later.

Third, I vowed not to stop taking my medication or visiting my therapist. We talked about common graces in chapter 6, and I made an agreement with myself not to step away from these common graces for any reason. Sometimes I think I'm doing well enough that I don't need my counselor anymore, and sometimes I think I can come off my medication. Now, this isn't true for everyone, but for me—someone with treatment-resistant depression and a strong history of suicidal ideations—it just isn't worth the risk. I have found a combination of things that is working for me. Why mess with something that's working, just so I can feel a little better about myself for not needing help to get through my days? It's not worth risking the stability I've gained.

Now, you might find yourself in a different situation than mine. I have a friend right now thinking about coming off his anxiety medication because he feels like he's stabilized and gained new coping skills during the eighteen months that he's been on meds. I encouraged him to talk with his physician about this to understand how to titrate effectively off his medication, or if it even makes sense to do so. I have another friend who was able to come off her antidepressants and antianxiety meds after being on them for about two years because she had done the hard work of identifying the root causes of her mental breakdowns. Each of us has a different path to walk regarding this, but for me, I need to stay on my meds. The risk of returning to uncontrolled suicidality simply remains too high.

What I Learned

I found myself filled with gratitude over the changes in my life when my pastor texted me. Armed with the above-mentioned tools, I have survived several years since my suicide attempt, but it's more than just survival—I'm thriving. I don't struggle every time July rolls around on the calendar. Instead, it's just another hot summer month in the desert for me. But I don't take this for granted because it's been the result of a lot of hard work by me and others.

I'm grateful to God for giving me safe people to be transparent with about my mental health struggles. My friends don't get aggravated with me or think less of me when I'm battling, but instead they rise up every time and support me. I wouldn't be here today without them, and I know God brought these friends into my life. I know that not everyone has five or six people who they can reach out to when things start to go astray, and I feel so blessed to have these folks in my community. I praise God that I uncovered the simple morning routine that gets me centered every day. I've even gotten to the point where I get up extra early to maintain that pattern if necessary. One time recently, my wife and I caught an airplane that left at six in the morning, so I voluntarily got up at three thirty to have time for my morning routine. To top it all off, I wasn't even grumpy about having to get up early—talk about your miracles!

Beyond gratefulness, I have learned that it's important for me to stay humble and dependent upon God. Something unexpected could hit my life that would turn it upside down. The only way forward, the only way to stay healthy, is to not rely on my own strength. This sounds cliché, but I really have learned that my strength pales in comparison to God's grandeur, and I'm far better off trusting him to manage the big problems in my life than depending upon myself. After all, there has never been a moment when God sat up in heaven saying, "Oh no! I didn't see that one coming. What shall I do? I'm stumped." God knows the beginning of all things from the end of all things. Best to lay my struggles at his feet and let him address them as he sees fit. This continues to be a challenge for me because I've lived a good portion of my life depending on my own strength and intelligence to get through the unexpected things. And if I'm honest, I thought I did a pretty good job of managing those surprises. But I remind myself regularly that I was also ignoring my emotions during those stressful seasons. I stuffed my depression away and acted as though I had everything sorted when nothing could be further from the truth. In other words, I wasn't doing such a great job after all.

Why It Matters

God longs for all of us to find our groove like I have. He desires for each of us to overcome our unhealthy habits and find our truest selves in him. But getting there will cost us literally everything. In John 12:25, Jesus said, "Those who love their life in this world will lose it. Those who care nothing for their life in this world will keep it for eternity." What does this have to do with rediscovering your own groove, you might ask? Quite simply, everything. There is only one way to live life to its fullest, and that's living the way that God intended humans to live in the first place. God doesn't want us to build an existence separate from him but rather to live in dependence upon him. A divine exchange happens when we stop relying on our own wisdom and strength to survive in life. Instead, we cease trying altogether. We give up and give in to God, relying on him and his strength.

Isaiah 40:28–31 contains a beautiful image of this exchange:

> Have you never heard? Have you never understood? The LORD is the everlasting God, the Creator of all the earth. He never grows weak or weary. No one can measure the depths of his understanding. He gives power to the weak and strength to the powerless. Even youths will become weak and tired, and young men will fall in exhaustion. But those who trust in the LORD will find new strength. They will soar high on wings like eagles. They will run and not grow weary. They will walk and not faint.

What a profound declaration of the majesty of God and his intentions toward us. Our God created all things. He never gets tired, and he empowers those who are weary or feel powerless. My favorite part of this passage has always been where those who trust

> *Our God created all things. He never gets tired, and he empowers those who are weary or feel powerless.*

in the Lord will find new strength. The Hebrew word translated as *find* actually means *exchange*. In context then, the promise of God states that we can exchange our weakness for his strength, our powerlessness for his power. What a deal!

Romans 5 gives us another view of how God works to help us regain our groove. The apostle Paul talks about the good fruit of difficult times, which includes endurance, strength of character, and confident hope. Then in verse 5 he says, "And this hope will not lead to disappointment. For we know how dearly God loves us, because he has given us the Holy Spirit to fill our hearts with his love." God has given us the Holy Spirit as proof of his love and as a demonstration of the fact that we can stand strong in our sense of hope. In today's world, we often think of hope as a weak word. We might hope our favorite baseball team wins the World Series, or we might hope our parents call us back after years of ignoring us, but this hope feels a lot like the word *wish*. This isn't the type of hope Paul speaks about. He says we can know God's love exists for us because of the evidence of the Holy Spirit within us. We can trust that our difficulties will result in a good turn of events because God has given us the Holy Spirit. This hope is a defiant, confident belief that things will get better, a hope that inspires us to rediscover our groove.

How It Applies

1. What would a meaningful morning routine look like for you? Would it be better for you to have a routine in the afternoon or evening rather than the morning?

2. What friends do you have right now who you can confide in when the going gets rough? If you can't think of anyone, consider talking to your pastor or another spiritual leader as a starting point (if they demonstrate the characteristics of being safe).

3. How much do you struggle with the idea of medications or therapy being common graces we should take advantage of? Does either one have baggage for you?

4. How difficult do you find it to be focused on gratitude, both when things are difficult and when things are starting to go well in your life?

5. Is humility a natural response for you, or are you more likely to want to take credit for all the things going right in your life?

What God Thinks

O God, You *are* my God; early will I seek You; my soul thirsts for You; my flesh longs for You in a dry and thirsty land where there is no water.

Psalm 63:1 NKJV

Too often when we come across verses like this, we focus on the "early" part. That's not really the emphasis, though. No, the emphasis should be on thirsting and longing for the presence of God in a parched place. So let's ask the tough question. Are you hungry and thirsty for more of God in your life? This remains perhaps the number one key to regaining your groove, because only God can set our lives back on the right track. It doesn't necessarily take five hours of praying on our knees to reorient our lives to God. Like me, you can do it in twenty minutes with some dedicated and focused time that is prioritized over everything else in your life. If you work the night shift, seeking God early in the morning might

152

be a waste of time; for you, midafternoon probably makes a lot more sense. Maybe you're not a morning person and you need your coffee before you can focus on anything. That's fine—just dedicate some time to reconnecting with and reorienting your life around God. The reward will be worth it, I promise.

15

Helping Others Along the Path

Be kind and compassionate to one another, forgiving each other, just as in Christ God forgave you.

Ephesians 4:32 NIV

My Story

All of a sudden, I started crying in the middle of my sermon. I wasn't prepared for this, but I guess I shouldn't have been surprised. This was, after all, the first time I had ever talked about my suicide attempt to anyone outside my inner circle. I got choked up when talking about when the Holy Spirit spoke to me. I couldn't get the words out, the ones that said, "You can't love me. I don't even love me." It felt as though I was right back in the psych ward with God speaking to me all over again, it seemed so fresh and tender. I apologized, grabbed a tissue, and tried to compose myself. For a good minute, I felt the warm tears stream down my face, and I just let them come. I could do nothing until I got through this moment. Finally, the tears subsided, and I finished my sentence. "You can't love me. I don't even love me." I looked at the youth group and added, "That's the first moment in years that I felt hope well up in my soul. If God wasn't going to stop loving me, maybe I could still be redeemable, even though I had attempted suicide."

I started my four-week sessions with the youth group in this way, as we talked about the reality of mental health in the world today. I didn't pull any punches with these young adults because they're already living it anyway. Bullies are a part of everyone's existence. Social pressures to live up to everyone's expectations are unrelenting. At least half the youth attending already had a mental health diagnosis, trying to figure out what God thought of them because of this damaging information. So I started with my story, to gain their trust. I needed them to know that I had been through the wringer too, just like them. I shared how my faith started out of suicidality and it never left me, no matter how unspiritual I felt or acted.

Then we moved into the life-giving comfort offered by God to everyone. We talked about how God knows all our secrets, even the ones we try to hide from our closest friends, and yet he still chooses us and loves us. I shared with them the idea that having other people who believe in them becomes a powerful antidote to the unyielding negativity that often surrounds them. Four weeks later, we ended our time together with a powerful object lesson. I asked for a brave volunteer to come to the front of the room and sit on a stool. Then I asked the group to answer three questions about this person:

1. What is this person good at?
2. When you think of this person, what do you think of?
3. What is God proud of this person for?

In every case, the group started off with some jokes or silliness. "Sam is good at being the butt of everyone's jokes." But then things got real, fast. Answers came out like, "I know I can trust Susannah with the hard things in my life, and she will pray for me while keeping my secret." Or "God is proud of Isaiah because he's a fierce warrior. He's had some heavy stuff come at him already in his life, but he never backs down, he never gives up, and he never quits." Some of the youth started to cry as they heard the truth of God spoken into their hearts, maybe for the first time in a long time or perhaps ever. Through smiles, tears came down almost everyone's face as they received the truths of their peers.

Then something unexpected happened, and the youth group asked if they could "do me." I sat in the chair and listened as these young adults spoke words of kindness and truth into my life. I heard them tell me that I must be a patient parent because I listen so well to them. They told me I taught well and knew the heart of God for broken people. They suggested that I should preach to the church in larger groups than just the youth group and that I should figure out what that looks like for me. Stunned by the depth and care these young adults displayed for me after having known me in most cases for only a few weeks, I barely held it together emotionally.

Since this guest-speaking session, I have had multiple youths come up to me and ask when I would return. I had one dad ask if his daughter could spend some time with me one-on-one in a safe environment to ask some more questions because she didn't get all the answers she wanted. The youth leaders have encouraged me to pursue more opportunities to speak about mental health in our church and in other places, because my message resounds with truth and power. In short, I went in with the intention to be a blessing to the youth group and teach them some things about mental health and faith—and I accomplished my mission—but I unexpectedly ended up being blessed by the youth group too.

What I Learned

When I began my journey with faith and mental health, I didn't have any vision or expectation of being able to help others along their own path toward wholeness. I just wanted to survive (most of the time anyway, some days that wasn't even true). Never in my wildest dreams would I have imagined that I might be someone who could speak to issues of mental health and faith. First, I honestly never imagined I would be healthy enough to be worth listening to. I assumed that I would always be struggling in one way or another. Beyond that, I still felt in my heart of hearts that my mental health diagnoses disqualified me from any true leadership role in any church or church event. So, I learned that God's intentions are often far grander than we can even imagine. That's a good thing because it means he calls us beyond ourselves and into something greater.

One of my friends—Lindsay—said something to me once that has stuck with me. She said that healthy friendships have give-and-take. Sometimes we are in a season where we need to take a lot of energy and attention from our friends because we aren't healthy or our circumstances just stink, and that's okay. Other times we are in a healthy space, and we are able to give out of our abundance to our friends who need help. This kind of ebb and flow has been true of my friendship with Lindsay over the years, but as I taught the youth group, I learned that this remains true of lives in general.

Some seasons require us to be in spiritual intensive care units, where we receive all sorts of specialized attention and care to keep us on life support. But eventually, we recover and regain health. Over time, we become the ones who administer the care to others, often in exactly the same situations we used to be stuck in. God has a way of redeeming our dark times for ministry circumstances. So, I found that I could minister out of a place of strength to the very things that used to be weaknesses for me because God has shored up my weaknesses and turned them into strengths. I will walk carefully, to make sure that I don't fall back into old patterns, but there are some things that are sealed up and will never reoccur in my life.

Why It Matters

God is in the business of rescuing lost people and restoring us to our intended use. This is his specialty, and he knows what we are built for even better than we know ourselves. A recurrent theme in the Psalms is for God to return, rescue, and restore the psalmist. One example can be found in Psalm 6:4—"Return, O LORD, and rescue me. Save me because of your unfailing love." Like the psalmist, we can cry out to God to return to us, rescue us, and save us. All because of his unending love for us. We may or may not have a vision for what that rescue or salvation looks like. More often than not, what we envision may be an unchanged us in better circumstances, but that isn't how God works. He's always looking to change us into the best version of ourselves, the version that most closely resembles Jesus.

Romans 12:2 says, "Don't copy the behavior and customs of this world, but let God transform you into a new person by changing the way you think. Then you will learn to know God's will for you, which is good and pleasing and perfect." Once God has rescued us, he gives us the opportunity to change the way we interact with our circumstances. Instead of letting our situations rule us, we can turn toward God and be transformed. This turn toward God will enable us to gain a clearer vision of what he has created us for in the first place. Once we uncover this, we will find God's will to

> *More often than not, what we envision may be an unchanged us in better circumstances, but that isn't how God works.*

be perfectly suited to our personalities, our experiences, our past challenges, and our current strengths. God perfectly fits each of us for service in accordance with who he created us to be and what we have previously lived out in our lives.

How It Applies

1. When did you last share your story in a way that encouraged others?
2. What are you good at?
3. When you think of yourself, what do you think of?
4. What is God proud of you for?
5. If you have a sense of what God's vision is for your life, what is that vision? (If you don't have that yet—it's okay. It will come, so start by asking God to show you.)

What God Thinks

All praise to God, the Father of our Lord Jesus Christ. God is our merciful Father and the source of all comfort. He comforts us in all our troubles so that we can comfort others. When they are troubled, we will be able to give them the same comfort God has given us.

2 Corinthians 1:3–4

Let's start this final God-centered moment by praising God for being the source of all comfort by undergoing a brief exercise. Imagine a life devoid of God and everything he brings into your life, and how empty it would feel. Now slowly reconsider all the different elements of life and hope that God gives you, and allow praise to rise in your spirit. Now it's time to remember the two reasons God gives us comfort. First, he loves us deeply and wants us to be comforted. Most of us are very comfortable with this idea, but it's the second idea that trips us up sometimes. God comforts us to allow us to comfort others. He wants us to be his literal arms so we can offer hugs and comfort to others who are going through it. Now it's time to put feet to this idea. Who do you know who needs comfort in their life that you can provide to them? What's keeping you from doing that today?

CONCLUSION

An Always Present God

As you've seen in this book, my life has been a roller coaster of ups and downs, with suicidality and depression writhing through most of my days. Rarely have I had a long season when I haven't felt the pull toward darkness. There have been moments when I've been able to withstand the temptation to move into that space, but I have always been aware of its draw. I know its appeal from the many times I have succumbed to its siren song. For long periods of my life, I joined the psalmists and cried for a seemingly absent God to make himself known because I found myself drowning in my torturous thoughts. I didn't see a way out, and if I'm being honest, I mostly blamed God for this. He is the all-powerful one, so why didn't he *do something* to fix this situation? As a matter of fact, why did he allow the circumstances in my life that set me on a path of suicidality and depression in the first place? This all could have been avoided if only God had intervened and been more present in my life.

I carried this undercurrent of frustration through most of my Christian experience. Even when things went well, I would wait for the other proverbial shoe to drop. I expected things to go sideways in my life sooner rather than later, and when something negative inevitably happened, I felt justified in my presumption of brokenness. And then once things started to unravel, I unraveled along with the circumstances because I didn't have the foundation to stand firm. This remained true despite the fact that I invested heavily in my spirituality, even getting a degree in biblical studies after graduating from high school. My volunteer activities at church didn't change this. I mentored young married couples and led small groups and evangelism efforts, but this piece of my spirit remained untouched. I never knew when suicidality or depression would raise its head again, and I felt unable to combat these things adequately because I didn't understand where they came from.

Now I see things differently than I used to, and I don't hold God responsible for the darkness that intruded upon my life as a youngster. I do wish that he would have prevented the terrible things I experienced from happening, but I live in this broken world. My pain, my depressive episodes, and my suicidality are some of the results. Now I have the privilege (no sarcasm intended) of working these things out with the Holy Spirit to find health and wholeness in my life. It's hard work, and some days are overwhelming still, but I know that I hold a lot of responsibility for my own mental health instead of only laying it all at God's feet.

It's on me to pay attention to the rhythms of my emotions and mental health, to pay attention to when things start to waver or feel just a bit off. If I notice that something isn't settling quite perfectly in my mind or emotions, I know now how to explore that off-kilter feeling. I know that I need to plumb the depths of my soul to figure out what's going on. I root out the source of the discontent and deeply consider it. Sometimes it's due to an unintentional distance between me and my wife or a friend, and I need to restore that relationship. Sometimes it's a function of sin taking hold of my heart, which means I need to confess it and ask God to cleanse my heart and mind through Jesus Christ. Sometimes I stray from the routines I have established for my daily life. I feel like I have outgrown those patterns and I don't need them to stay healthy, so I get lazy and let them fall by the wayside. This laziness invariably leads to problems, because I specifically set up these routines to keep myself on healthy paths. This intentionality and self-awareness have allowed me to let God off the hook with my mental health journey, alongside everything else we've discussed in this book. I hope that you've learned some ways to take responsibility for cultivating mental health in your own life too.

Let's talk a bit more about what I mean by letting God off the hook, though. He is the God of comfort, so he does have a role to play in our lives. I don't intend to say that God only helps those who help themselves, as I find statements like that unhelpful, unbiblical, and, frankly, dangerous. We are not the captains of our own lives, and we need to stay reliant upon the Holy Spirit to guide our daily decisions and habits. But at the same time, we can't step back from making the decisions that impact our daily activities because God hasn't told us exactly what to do. And, once we have understood a particular truth—whether that truth comes from the Bible or our psychotherapist—we have the responsibility to apply that truth to our lives. I think it's far too easy to look at the unfortunate and painful circumstances that have happened in our lives, choose to blame God for them, refuse to take responsibility for pursuing healing and wholeness, and instead stay wounded and incomplete. God calls us to more, and we have a part to play in achieving that more.

John 14:18 contains a powerful promise from Jesus. He says that he will never leave us as orphans in this world. We've discussed this verse briefly before, but it's worth revisiting as we close the book. Let's be honest—sometimes it feels like Jesus has left us as orphans, alone in a cold and dark world to face our trials on our own. My visits to the psych ward gave me a lot of time to consider the vignettes we walked through in this book at great length, and I learned something about God in retrospect as I thought back on these moments. In every instance, God was present in my life

> *God is always with you. It might feel like you're out there bat-tling life alone, but you aren't—God actively works with you for your freedom, joy, and maturity.*

despite the hardship. He never abandoned me, even when I accused him of doing just that. He didn't necessarily show up in the way I would have preferred, but he never bailed on me. That's a promise I want you to take away from this book too, that God is always with you. It might feel like you're out there battling life alone, but you aren't—God actively works with you for your freedom, joy, and maturity. What a strong promise to get you through dark times, if you'll only learn to hold tight to it instead of rail against it.

One final lesson I learned that has significantly changed the way I view God and his influence and presence in my life has to do with margins. I lived my life as though I needed to squeeze everything out of every moment available, and I left no room for margin. I often literally ran from work to church activities to fam-ily events and then fell into bed at the end of the day completely exhausted. This left no room for God's presence in my life, and that's a problem. God allows us to live life independently of him if we choose to because he never forces his way in. Often this can leave us living as practical atheists, where we technically believe in God but don't allow him to influence us in any meaningful way. When we have no margin, and when we leave no room for God to speak into our lives, then all it takes is one stray moment to knock us off course.

This happened to me many times, and I'm guessing it happens to you sometimes too. I've learned that margin becomes a powerful key to seeing the movement of God in my life, so I've made the very intentional decision to just slow down. My schedule isn't nearly as hectic as it used to be, and this is one-hundred-percent by design. Now I have the margin I need in my life to hear the direction and presence of God. That's another takeaway I'd like you to have from this book: build margin into your life. All the mindfulness routines and support groups and counseling and outreach to help others can be meaningless if you aren't connected to God as your source. While intimacy with God doesn't solve all of life's problems, it certainly gives you a different perspective on the events that happen in your life.

As you come to the end of this book, my hope and prayer are that you have been encouraged by my story of depression and suicidality. I want to end with the same promise I started with. God doesn't exclude anyone because of a mental health diagnosis or struggle. God specializes in working with broken humans. There is a grander portrait being painted with your life. In time, you will see that portrait, as I have been able to see it in my own life. Don't give up when times get dark, and don't give in to the lies that tell you it would be better if you weren't around. God loves you and is for you, always.

Maybe you've come to the end of this book and you're wondering what to do next. We've covered a *lot* of ground here, and it can be overwhelming to find a tangible next step in your journey toward mental wholeness. With that in mind, I've created a short video course on resilience especially for readers of this book. In the five sessions, we will cover a more detailed definition of resilience, where God fits into the picture of resilience, and where we can find resilience, among other topics. You can find a QR code for this video course in the *Additional Resources* section. I hope you'll take the time to learn more about resilience—trust me, it will be worthwhile!

ADDITIONAL RESOURCES

If you picked up this book, then it's likely you or someone you love has battled depression, suicidality, or other mental health conditions. It can be overwhelming to try to find faith-friendly, person-centered, God-honoring encouragement when this is the path you find yourself on. This is why I wrote *Resilient and Redeemed*, it's why I speak across the nation on mental health and faith, it's why I write articles on these topics, and it's near the center of my heart for ministry.

Reading a book like this hopefully stirs a sense of expectation that you or your loved one can persevere through the challenges life is bringing and that you're not *stuck* in the darkness for the rest of your life. In my experience, one of the keys to getting out of the shadows is resilience. It's so easy to just lie down and quit when we feel overwhelmed or overcome by emotions, circumstances, and mental health challenges. But resilience gives us the courage to stand back up, even if we're unsteady, and to strive for something better in our lives.

Because I believe in the power of resilience as a foundational truth to support us in our darkest days, I have created a video series on resilience specifically for readers of this book. Over the course of five videos, I cover the following topics:

- What is a working definition of resilience, and how does it apply to your spiritual journey?

- What are some tools that will allow you to access resilience in your own life?
- What does God have to do with resilience?
- Is resilience infinite, or is there a limit to its ability to support us?
- Where can we find resilience in the world?

If these topics sound appealing to you, I invite you to use the QR code below to access the course. There's no cost to you, and I don't ask for anything in return. I'd also like to invite you to join my newsletter list. I send out monthly emails that provide you with news on my upcoming book releases and give you practical, relevant information on how to maximize your mental health.

ChrisMorrisWrites.com/a-course-on-resilience/

ACKNOWLEDGMENTS

I have to start by thanking my wife for sticking with me. She's been through some dark times with me and has never given up on me. She saw the light and hope of Jesus through my mental health struggles long before I did and encouraged me to keep going.

Thank you to every one of my friends who has texted or called or Facebook messaged me through dark times. I wouldn't be here today without you. Kevin, Tim, and Joel—I'm looking especially at you as I say this.

Lindsay and Catherine, thanks for always pushing me to move forward with my writing. It seems like almost every day I'm talking to one or the other of you and you're telling me that I have a story to tell, one that people need to hear. I almost didn't turn in this proposal because I wasn't sure it would sell, but you both encouraged me to do it anyway because publishers don't ask for proposals they don't want to see. As usual, you were both right. Someday I will learn to trust your gut more than my own.

I also want to thank my agent extraordinaire, Mary DeMuth from Mary DeMuth Literary. You've been an inspiration and support in my life even before you were my agent. I remember telling my friends that I hope to write like you when I grow up.

I hope this book is the start of that journey. Thanks for believing in me.

Thank you as well to Andy McGuire, Elisa Haugen, and the entire team at Bethany House Publishers. I'm so honored that you saw a story worth telling in this book.

Chris Morris is a passionate mental health advocate dedicated to promoting better understanding of mental health issues within the church. Because of a lifelong struggle with depression and suicidality, Chris became committed to breaking down the stigma surrounding mental health and encouraging others to seek after holistic health.

As a writer and speaker, Chris has shared his personal story and insights with audiences across the country, inspiring many individuals to take control of their own health, break free from poor theological teaching placed upon them, and seek the support they need. He has published several books on mental health, and his work has been featured in a number of media outlets, including Crosswalk, The Mighty, and *Fathom* magazine.

Chris is deeply committed to creating a more compassionate and supportive world and church for individuals living with mental health issues. Through his writing and speaking, he is a powerful voice for change and a beacon of hope for those in need. Find out more at ChrisMorrisWrites.com.